LIFE IS A CIRCUS

4/25/03

To Craig:

May all your days continue to be happy Circus days.

Good luck

Shirley Carroll O'Connor

LIFE IS A CIRCUS

Shirley Carroll O'Connor

Library of Congress Number:		99-91850
ISBN #:	Hardcover	0-7388-1314-1
	Softcover	0-7388-1315-X

This book was printed in the United States of America.

To order additional copies of this book, contact:
Xlibris Corporation
1-888-7-XLIBRIS
www.Xlibris.com
Orders@Xlibris.com

CONTENTS

This book is dedicated to Kevin,
who has always been there for me;
to Donna, who is more than a daughter to me;
to Colin and Meghann, my two precious grandchildren
and to all my dear friends
for their unfailing support and love.

CHAPTER ONE

Not every bride who starts her honeymoon is accompanied by a real live leopard! I should have known then what my life would be like in the ensuing years, but I was naive.

It all began innocently enough. I met my future husband through a friend. She had invited me to her house to meet an old college beau who was with a touring circus spending the winter in Los Angeles. It wasn't the gentleman that I was interested in meeting, it was the fact that he was bringing his girlfriend who trained elephants!

My knowledge of circuses and elephants was very limited, and the idea of meeting a young woman who trained anything as gargantuan as an elephant was overwhelming. Actually, I remember very little about the girl elephant trainer; I was more intrigued with my friend's old flame, Norman Carroll. At the time Norman was a sideshow talker, or barker. He was also the Big Top announcer and Ringmaster. In addition, he announced the Wild West after show.

The occupations of these guests were unknown to me as I had only been to two circuses in my entire life. Once when I was about five years old in Cleveland, Ohio; and the the only thing I remember about that one was that there was a terrific rainstorm and we had to run for our lives for fear the tent would blow down. Then when I was in my late teens, an erstwhile boyfriend took me to Madison Square Garden in New York to see Ringling Brothers and Barnum & Bailey Circus. But, if I remember correctly, my escort was rather hard-pressed for cash so we sat up high in the balcony, behind a post, so neither of those recollections served to endear the circus to me.

The stories that Norman told that afternoon about the circus and the performers were fascinating. When he invited me to see the circus, I accepted with alacrity. Of course, the fact that he was six feet, three inches tall and very good looking, didn't have a thing to do with it!

The circus was Cole Brothers Circus, one of the large tented, touring railroad circuses, and it was at the tail end of a very long engagement in Los Angeles. It had been playing on the old circus lot at Washington and Hill Streets in downtown Los Angeles for about a month, and it was a pretty sorry sight. Not only was it the end of the local engagement, but it was just about the end of the season, and everything was tired—performers and equipment.

My impression was anything but favorable. When Norman invited us, I had asked a girlfriend and her little boy to accompany me to the circus, into the sideshow; I was both fascinated and repulsed. Many of the people I met that day later became my friends, but if someone had told me that would eventually be the case, I would have told them they had flipped their lids.

I remember, most vividly, one of the attractions, a hayseed of a character named "Little Abner". He was a tall, gawky young man, in his early twenties, dressed in overalls. His claim to fame was the fact that he could stuff a dozen golf balls into his mouth at one time! Ugh! I was so nauseated, I was ready to whoops.

Some of the other "attractions" included the Tattooed Lady, Betty Broadbent. In his sideshow pitch Norman used to say, "She has the Eiffel Tower on one shoulder and the Brooklyn Bridge on the other. Come in and see what's under construction . . . " I found out later that she had the tattooing done during the height of the depression because she had a child to support and there were no jobs.

Eko and Iko were the sheep-headed men from Ecuador! Actually, they were Negro albino twins with loads of wild-looking blond kinky hair. When one of them lost his hair, I remember Norman at the front of the sideshow saying, "Come in and see the sheep-headed men, one with a full head of grade A wool and the other in the process of molting!"

Sealo, the Seal Boy was born with flipper-like appendages where he should have had arms. Jose, the Armless Boy, was born without arms but could do anything with his feet. There were others: the Fat Lady, Alice from Dallas; the sword swallower who, some years later on a radio show, responded to an interviewer's question about how she took up sword swallowing said, "Oh you know, monkey see, monkey do!"

In the days before medicine made great strides in preventing some of these "Freaks of Nature", the sideshows provided a safe and acceptable haven for those who would have been shunned by society. As an example, I remember a conversation I had with Sam Alexander, the "Two-Faced Man". Sam had an accident when he was in his early twenties. He was cleaning out an old empty gas tank, and made the mistake of lighting a match. He received deep burns around his lips which became infected. The infection spread ending with the doctors having to make deeper cuts that took away the areas around the mouth and nose leaving him with half a face. After thirteen months in the hospital, he was discharged to what they called the "County Farm", a facility primarily for indigents who had no hope of recovery. He was fortunate to meet a lady doctor whose husband made prostheses and she made arrangements for Sam to see him. The result was a facial mask, that in the right light, looked like a real face.

Sam felt the only way he could get away from the "County Farm" was to get a job, but where and doing what. He remembered seeing a large carnival with a sideshow on his trip to pick up his mask, and he managed to get to the manager, who brushed him off with a curt "Whad'ya want?" Whereupon Sam replied, "Well, I can take my face off and put it back on again." After the manager recovered from the shock, Sam had a job and a life again.

When asked what would have happened to him if he hadn't gone into the sideshow, he replied, "I probably would have ended my days in an institution." He went on to say, "A whole new world opened up for me. I belonged. I was independent and that feeling was shared by all the so-called "freaks" who, like me, would have been warehoused in institutions or hidden away by their relatives."

If I wasn't impressed with the sideshow, I was even less impressed with the Big Show. In fact, I have only two memories of that event. One was an exciting discovery. It was my first awareness of the art of clowning, and it was provided by a man who was one of the greatest artists of pantomime, Otto Griebling.

Otto was known as a "tramp" clown. He was a past master of the art of clowning, which in essence is that art of aping the absurdity of the human condition. He ended his career with Ringling Brothers and Barnum & Bailey Circus at over seventy, and after having experienced serious operations for a vocal disorder, he was still tops for my money.

I learned later there are three basic types of clowns. The most familiar is the classical "Whiteface". The conventional Whiteface is recognized by his frilly white, usually sequined costume. The "Carpet Clown" evolved into the "Tramp" clown, and the "Auguste" uses costumes and makeup that exaggerate. Variations have sprung from the three basic types. "Whiteface" divided into "Neat" and "Auguste", the slapstick specialist, who makes us laugh just by looking at him.

I considered the clowns some of my best friends as I really got to know them. I found that contrary to popular opinion, they were not sad, unhappy people hiding behind makeup, but instead were bright, creative people who really cared about bringing happiness to others.

Among my favorites, besides Otto Griebling, were Lou Jacobs, Felix Adler, Bobby Kay, Mark Anthony, Bill Ballantine, Albert White, Chuck Burnes and Emmett Kelly.

The other memory was the finale of the circus. In those days it was the tradition to close the circus performance with what was called, "living statues".

This holdover from the turn of the century, or even before, may have created a sensation in that era when the gilded or whitewashed figures, human and animal, posed motionless in a series of tableaux that depicted such dramatic subjects as "The Rainbow Fountain", "The Dance of Life", "Victory", or the "Spirit of Flight".

But in 1943, at the end of the season, it was a mess. I don't remember what the title of the opus was, but I do remember that the performers' wigs were askew, and the supposed marble whiteness of the costumes was more than slightly mud-colored.

Years later in a conversation with Betty Escalante, one of the "living statues", she told me, "We wore a little ditty belt here and a little tit-holder and a cap. We put alboline on, then a gold powder they used for painting radiators and you had to take it off with more alboline and cheese cloth. In hot weather there was one bucket of water for six people. You didn't have time to rot because you had to rush to get into costumes for the next number. You glittered every time the sun hit you and the next day everyone knew who was sleeping with whom because they'd all be glittering!"

In later years it got easier after they found a white-based liquid from Max Factor that was painted on and could be sponged off. In Cole Brothers Circus, they worked with an old white horse that could pose. It knew the minute the curtain went up and it never moved.

My impression of the circus left much to be desired. I left the lot that afternoon with no inclination to repeat the experience in the near future. Of course, I couldn't say the same about seeing Norman Carroll; but it was highly unlikely that I would be seeing him again because the circus was moving on and Norman with it.

The circus became a vague memory until one day the following December, fourteen months later, when I received a call. Norman was back in town for the holidays and would I have dinner with him. Would I? Wild horses couldn't stop me!

CHAPTER TWO

Norman's mother and brother had moved to Los Angeles from Oklahoma city, and he had come to spend the holidays with them. They had found a little frame house out near the old Seelig Zoo, the winter quarters for various circus performers. The house was tiny and was in the rear of another house, but in those war years, it was a real *coup* to have found any place to live.

It was located near the end of a streetcar line, and a real plus because this was the time of gas rationing, and even if you were lucky enough to have a car, unless you were in a war-essential work, you didn't have the necessary gas stamps available to run it.

Norman Carroll O'Connor (somehow the O'Connor was dropped when Norman entered show business; his version was that the only good review he got left off the "O'Connor" and being a superstitious Irishman, "Carroll" was it) was the eighth child in a family of thirteen. He was born in Vincennes, Indiana, the son of Sarah and William O'Connor. He lived there until he was seven years old, and nothing in that early childhood indicated that the circus would become his life.'

In these days of delving into everyone's psyche, an explanation of his love for and with the circus could possibly be explained by the fact that the O'Connors lived on Main Street, the route of the traditional Circus Parade.

To a little boy, with a flair for the dramatic, the circus parade with its riotous color, its magnificent and awe-inspiring animals, its beautiful ladies in exotic costumes, its comical clowns and its ear-splitting, soul-stirring calliope music, was bound to make an unforgettable subliminal impression. But the circus, on the conscious level, couldn't compete with the fact that his father, an oil man, who was involved in drilling oil wells in Oklahoma and decided to move his family west. Norman's mind was filled with visions of Indians and the wild west, and that is just what the family found they had moved into.

They spent three years in Sapulpa, Oklahoma, right in the heart of Indian territory. They rented a house on Indian land from an oil-rich Indian. Norman's playmates were Indian boys and girls, and while he didn't realize it at the time, he was living right in the middle of a Wild West Circus.

From Sapulpa, the family moved to Oklahoma City. As Irish Catholics, the family's life revolved around the church, and so it was only natural that ten-year-old Norman was drafted to serve as an acolyte at Mass. Norman loved the ceremony and solemnity of the services and the High Masses. To his youthful mind, the cassocks and surplices the priests and altar boys wore were costumes. Even Latin was easy for him; it was like learning his part in a play, and he played it with all the zeal of a Barrymore.

The sacred processions were a particular delight to Norman, and secretly he referred to them as "parades". It was only in later years that he convinced himself that such a reference was not sacrilegious.

Thirteen children in those depression days created quite a problem. Work was scarce for father O'Connor, and it was either feast or famine. It was only natural that all the children found some kind of work to supplement the family income.

Norman's many occupations ran the gamut of newspaper boy, delivering weighty boxes of groceries for fifty cents a week, caddying at a local golf course, working at the County Fair, and eventually ending up as a Master of Ceremonies in a local "beer joint". He earned quite a reputation as a "clown", and it was at this point that fate stepped in, in the person of Uncle Leo Blondin.

"Uncle" Leo had been a circus clown in his youth, and even though at this stage of his life he was the curator of the Oklahoma City Zoo, his love of the circus never left him. In young Norman, Uncle Leo found an avid listener to stories about the circus, and with his natural inclinations for the dramatic, it wasn't long before he developed an all-consuming desire to join a circus.

In the meantime Uncle Leo initiated him into the art of clown makeup, and Norman developed what he thought was a very funny clown character called "Tumpsey". He volunteered to don the grease paint at the drop of a hat for parades, parties, or what have you. Uncle Leo still had friends in the circus world, and he promised the young "Joey" (circus parlance for "clown") that he would write to these friends about a job for Norman. Sure enough, he received a reply from Russell Brothers Circus, and was offered fifteen dollars a week to clown and make himself "generally useful". A term used for doing any dirty job like putting up and tearing down the seats.

Russell Brothers Circus was owned by Pauline and Claude Webb, two very colorful characters. Coming from the hills of Tennessee, they had managed to acquire the circus, and in 1934 when Norman joined, it was a fairly successful "Sunday School", (no gambling) truck show. He wasn't there a week before Pauline found out that he wasn't a very good clown. Apparently the only laughs he got were from the other clowns. She did see, he had potential however, and first made him a ticket taker, then side show barker and finally Big Show announcer.

He liked telling about his early years on the show, when he slept in a pup tent with his feet sticking out, or about driving the girls' "sleeping" truck and because the girls didn't trust him not to fall asleep,after he had hit a "pig" truck & knocked them all out of bed, they got the snake charmer and her snakes to ride in the cab with him.

Another memory was of Pauline Webb's very large family falling out of the hills to visit the circus. There were so many that Pauline pinned tags on them so they wouldn't get clipped by the concessionaires. Norman remembered vividly one of the group eating in the cookhouse and when told it was going to close, his saying, "I ain't leaving here 'til I get my gut filled!"

One of his special memories was about a little midget, Charles

Del Rio, in the sideshow who would do a "shuffle off to Buffalo" dance and because he was usually drunk would fall off his stand into the arms of some girl. Pauline hired Norman, at $2.00 a week to keep him from drinking. They would go shopping in the five & ten cent stores, his favorite place because he could duck between the counters and lose Norman and head for the nearest bar. When Norm would start canvassing the bars the midget would have already told everyone that a great big hulking guy was coming after him and that he was a slave driver. Norman would barely get out without being lynched

Another time as he was announcing the "SPEC", the parade of all the performers, he noticed a strange tall dark Indian Squaw walking past him and with a start realized it was Pauline. He said, "My God what are you doing?" and she yelled, "Shut up I'm hiding from a subpoena server", but she couldn't resist counting the house!

There was no need for Norman to run away and join the circus. His mother even helped him pack his trunk. After all, that was one less mouth to feed. I really doubt that was the case, but I'm sure mother O'Connor felt that Norman's soul needed to be fed by experiencing firsthand the wonders of show business. Maybe she felt that this experience would cure him of such a career desire and that he would come home and settle into a nice respectable job.

If this was truly her hope, she was in for some disappointment, because not only did he fall in love with the circus, but it became his life. In all fairness to mother O'Connor, that wonderful lady did all in her power to encourage him as he advanced from Russell Brothers Circus to Cole Brothers Circus to Pollock Brothers, Clyde Beatty, and finally to the big one—Ringling Brothers and Barnum & Bailey Circus.

On that day in December when Norman called me for a dinner date, I was up to my ears in war work. I was working for one of the War Chest agencies as an assistant executive director. The agency was Russian War Relief. In those days, Russia was our ally, and the Board of Directors boasted of some of the top leaders in religion, science, the arts and the civic community. During the time that I worked there, the presidents of the organization in Los Angeles included such fine conservative men as Justice Thomas P. White of the State Court of Appeals and Federal Judge Pierson M. Hall.

My position was actually in the field of Public Relations, but that field was still relatively new, and even I didn't know that organizing a speakers bureau and helping to stage large events and concerts at the Hollywood Bowl fell into that category. Up until I joined Russian War Relief, I had held a number of jobs, none that really qualified me for the position. In fact, I was originally hired as a bookkeeper to replace a casual acquaintance of mine who was leaving to have a baby.

At the time, I was working in a defense plant as a cost accountant. How I got that job I'll never know, because to this day I can't add two and two without the aid of an calculator. I never cease to wonder at the ability of this nation to win World War II with incompetents like me contributing patriotically to our war effort. I was young then, and while I wasn't noted for my looks or any great talents, I didn't have to take a back seat to anyone when it came to getting by on sheer nerve.

My background was as different from Norman's as night and day. I was born Shirley Rose Horn in Cleveland, Ohio, the youngest of four children—in fact, nine years younger than my sister, Gertrude, and sixteen years younger than my sister Leah. My only brother, Wally, was fourteen years older, so in essence, it was almost like being an only child. By the time I was old enough to really be aware of my siblings, they had left the nest and were trying their wings out in the world.

My father, Max Horn, was born in Austria. He was a handsome, delightful man with sparkling blue eyes and a real zest for life. He had only one fault. He was so naive that he trusted everyone. As an example he bought a new Buick and hired a driver to teach him how to drive and that was the last we saw of the Buick & the driver!

My mother, Fannie Weisberg Horn, came from proud Hungarian stock. She was born in New York City in 1882, and in her youth was considered one of the most beautiful young women ever to grace that city.

While my parents came from fairly religious Jewish families, they did not attend any synagogue, nor were we ever given any formal religious training. The first time I was in a synagogue was for my sister Gert's wedding when I was twelve. To the day he died, my brother would break down and cry (when he had a few too many) because he was never *bar mitzvahed.* But in spite of our seeming laxity in not belonging to a temple, or because my mother believed it was more important to go to school than to stay home on holidays, we really were a religious family in that we adhered to the ten commandments, and our motto was, "Live and let live".

My mother and father may have come from the same religious background, but in reality, they came from different worlds, and in those days family counselors and psychologists were either unknown or unaffordable.

Instead, Mama and Papa were always separating. Of course, they always went back together because they really loved one another, but it didn't take much for Mama to pick up and head east to New York or Chicago, or west to California; and naturally Mama would take me.

In twelve years of schooling, I went to twelve schools, from one end of the country to the other.

CHAPTER THREE

The old saying that opposites attract must certainly have some validity because Norman and I were just that. Our backgrounds were poles apart—our religions, educations and most of all, our current environments. But Norman was tall and handsome, and that combined with a 4-F status during the war wasn't the easiest to come by. Also, he was one of the nicest men I had met in a long time. A rarity, in that day and age, because like most men I had met, he didn't try to talk me into going to bed with him on the first date.

We didn't get to see too much of each other because he lived on the northeast side of Los Angeles, I lived in Hollywood, and it was a good two-hour streetcar ride away.

Our second date was an invitation to a New Year's Eve party at his friend's house in east Los Angeles. I really didn't give too much consideration to this being a serious relationship until the night he invited me to that New Year's Eve party at the Escalantes.

The Escalantes were a Mexican circus family, and it seemed to me then that there were a million of them. Papa and Mama Escalante lived in a little frame house in the Boyle Heights section of town. The house had only three small bedrooms, but the yard contained house trailers of all sizes and shapes plus flying act and other circus equipment. The Escalantes were top aerialists, as well as all-around performers.

There were always children in the house because as the older Escalantes would go out on the road with various circuses, Mama would inherit the care of the school-age youngsters who remained at home.

The night of the party, we had come all the way from Hollywood, a good hour and a half ride on the streetcar, with me dressed in a formal. You can imagine how chagrined I was to find myself in one of the more run-down sections of town (even the sidewalks weren't paved) all dressed to kill. I was also pretty disgusted with Norman for dragging me all that way on a streetcar for what I was sure was going to be a real bust of an evening.

I couldn't have been more wrong. From the moment that the door of that modest dwelling was opened, we were made to feel welcome. Norman was like one of the family, and the reception I received put me at complete ease. I can't remember ever having had a better time.

Mama Escalante promptly engaged me in a conversation. The only problem was that she only spoke Spanish, and I only spoke English, but believe it or not, and this continued as long as mama lived, we understood one another.

It was a bang-up night. The entire Escalante family were warm, loving, generous people—the men handsome, the women gorgeous, and the children beautiful. The fact that the house was crowded, as was the backyard, only served to add to the warmth. I especially remember Phil and Betty, Blackie and Lorena, Esther, Milonga and Lalo, and of course, mama and papa Escalante. It wasn't until the wee hours of the morning that we boarded the streetcar for the long trek back to Hollywood. Somehow, with the aid of tequila and the memory of the warm friendship, the ride didn't seem but half as long.

My regard for Norman after that evening really grew. I reasoned that anyone who had such wonderful friends had to have some pretty great things going for him. Our succeeding few dates found us discovering that we really did have things in common. We both loved good art and good literature, and we had fun in each other's company.

It isn't hard to fall in love when you have a common meeting ground and all the basic essentials. When Norman asked me to marry him, it certainly didn't take me very long, at the age of 27 (in those days considered being close to "old maid" status), to make up my mind to say yes.

Our original plans called for us to get married on February 20th, and my good friend and boss, Martha Lord, was going to have a reception for us. I had received word that my mother was arriving from the east, and inasmuch as I had a one-room apartment that I was subletting, the only way to get one at that time, she would be staying with me. Obviously, you couldn't have a mother and a husband in a one-room apartment, so we had to find a place for mother before we could get married.

Not too thrilled about my forthcoming marriage because she assumed she would be living with me, mama arrived, and as luck would have it she found what she hoped would be pleasant living quarters. So, the road was clear.

Now it was time to meet my prospective in-laws. Norman was a great believer in using reverse psychology, and he had drawn a vivid picture of both his mother and brother that had me quaking in my shoes. Somehow my prospective mother-in-law, in my mind, took on the image of a Grant Wood painting. I pictured her with thin, tight lips, and a stern, forbidding expression. I knew she was a devout Catholic, and I had been led to believe that she frowned upon drinking, smoking and any type of frivolity.

As the day approached for our meeting, I was terrified. My mother and I (I most certainly needed her for moral support) were invited to Sunday dinner. I managed to borrow a car, thanks to the kindness of some friends who were affluent enough to have a car and gas stamps, and was spared the two-hour ride on the streetcar.

As it was, I was a bundle of nerves. The prospect of meeting my future in-laws had already made me a basket case and I was justifiably nervous at the prospect of borrowing such a valuable item as a car! My fears were allayed somewhat when the trip across town proceeded without incident; that is, until we pulled up to Norman's address and I tried to turn the car around.

I had no sooner had it blocking the entire narrow street when "boom", the car backfired and the motor proceeded to die. In my anxiety, I managed to flood the darn thing, and there we were stuck with cars honking furiously at us. After five minutes of this, my mother could take no more, and she decided to ring the doorbell and send him out to help. It took Norman and several neighbors about ten minutes to get the car properly parked; but my big concern was not about the car, it was about how my mother was faring with my prospective mother-in-law.

When Norman took my arm and propelled me to the door, and I needed propelling because my legs suddenly seemed to be made of jelly, I was almost numb with fear. The door opened, and there stood Mrs. O'Connor, a tall, heavy-set, happy-faced woman, drink in hand, welcoming me warmly into her house. You can imagine my surprise when I found that both she and my mother were not only having a ball together, but they were also slightly looped!

It seems my mother-in-law had promptly offered a drink to my mother, who readily accepted, and mother O'Connor poured them both a brandy. This in itself wasn't enough to make them high, but mother O'Connor had used hollow-stemmed champagne glasses and neither of them was feeling any pain.

Needless to say, all my fears were groundless. I have never been able to understand the problems that some daughters-in-law seem to have with their mothers-in-law. My mother-in-law was very close to me for over 24 years, and her memory is one I treasure.

There was only one more obstacle to overcome—money! It was off-season, and Norman was broke, and I had a tremendous savings account of $200, which was hardly enough to start married life. As fate would have it, we had stopped at the Biltmore Hotel Bar for a drink one night before going to the Orpheum Theater to see a vaudeville show, one of Norm's favorite pastimes. There, we ran into Art Concello of Russell Brothers-Pan Pacific Circus. Norman introduced me, and told him we were about to be married. That caused no end of talk among the group of circus people at Mr. Concello's table, and bets were laid that the marriage wouldn't last six weeks. I didn't know then that Norman had a reputation of being the playboy of the circus world.

How he managed to get $50 from Art Concello, I'll never know. Maybe he borrowed it, and if that was the case, I'm sure Mr. Concello was amply repaid; or maybe it was a wedding gift. At any rate, we figured that was the extra bit we needed to start married life.

On the way to the theater we made a big decision. We wouldn't wait until the 20th, and anyhow we were both too scared to face a big reception, so we decided to get married the next day. True, we had our blood tests, but we didn't have a ring, and it would mean finding a judge to marry us—rounding up witnesses, our mothers, etc. The ring problem was solved at a little junk store next to the Orpheum where we found matching gold-filled rings for $5 each, which after a short time turned green.

A telephone call to Justice Thomas P. White brought forth a promise that he would be delighted to marry us the next afternoon at 2:00 p.m. in his chambers. We had chosen to ask Justice White, rather than any of the other judges I knew, because he was a leading Catholic layman, and we thought that was the very least we could do for Norman's mother, inasmuch as we weren't going to have a religious ceremony.

I don't think I've experienced many such hectic days. I didn't even have a proper dress, so early in the morning of February 6, 1945, I rushed down to the Broadway Hollywood and found something that I thought appropriate, although it later turned out to be the one color that Norman detested. Then I rounded up two friends to be our witnesses, and I was as ready as I would ever be.

My affluent friend who had loaned me her car on that memorable occasion also lent me her fur coat to wear, and was nice enough to drive me down to the Hall of Records where I was to meet Norman. My mother and the witnesses were to meet us in Justice White's chambers at the appointed hour.

Well, there I stood outside of that old building waiting for my bridegroom. Five minutes went by, ten minutes, and I was beginning to feel like the bride that's been left at the church. But, left at the Hall of Records, that was ridiculous!

Fifteen minutes and no Norman. Just at the point when I was ready to chuck the whole thing, I spotted him high-tailing it up Broadway, a small paper sack in hand, with his mother trailing behind him about ten paces.

Seems that they had gone downtown a little early because Norman needed to pick up a few things. In the process, they passed a store where people were waiting in line, and in those war years you got in any line because it was more than likely that you needed whatever they were selling. That particular line was for men's underwear.

If one had any doubts about the advisability of getting married, applying for a license in the old Los Angeles Hall of Records was almost enough to convince you that it wasn't a very good idea. The clerks seemed to be crotchety old people who couldn't care less about young or even old lovers. In fact, the whole atmosphere was pretty dismal. But we managed to get through all the necessary details and finally headed for the State Building and Justice White's chambers.

The ceremony, what I remember of it, was very nice because Justice White was a wonderful, kind man, and he had written something just a little special for us. But I'm sure we both stood there thinking, what in the devil have we gotten ourselves into now!

After the wedding, we had a drink at the Biltmore Hotel, and then Norman, my mother and I went back to my apartment by cab. Mama was moving out, and Norm was moving in, and thus started our honeymoon.

CHAPTER FOUR

The next day dawned bright and crisp and clear. We didn't have enough money to really go away on a honeymoon, so a trip to Arrowhead Springs that day was going to suffice.

Norman was very active in organizing U.S.O. shows during the war. His 4-F status was a constant source of unhappiness to him, and he had tried every means to get into some branch of the service, any branch, but with no luck. It seems he had a double hernia from having lifted some heavy props in his early circus days, and unless he had an operation, and even then it was doubtful, the services wouldn't take him. Hence his activity with the U.S.O.

The trip to Arrowhead Springs Hotel, which was then a rest center for the Navy, had been planned some time in advance, and Norm had gotten a number of acts together for the show. A Red Cross station wagon was to pick us up. Sure enough, at 8:00 a.m., the station wagon honked, and it was a mad rush to get out of the apartment. Consequently, with all the dashing, I just slid into the front seat next to the driver, and Norman sat next to the door.

I didn't notice if there was anyone in the back seat, and as we took off, I was surprised to hear Norman say, "Darling, I want you to meet one of my very dear friends." With that, I turned around, prepared to give his friend my very warmest smile, when my smile froze. There, about six inches from my face, was the biggest, snarliest leopard I had ever seen in my entire life. In fact, the only leopard I had ever seen outside of a zoo! It seems Norman's dear friend was Olga Celeste, known throughout the circus world as "The Leopard Lady".

I'm sure I must have aged a good twenty years in that few moments. Just imagine coming face to face with what is known as the most treacherous of all cats! This particular specimen weighed over 200 pounds, and it was draped across Olga Celeste's lap.

Her name was "Nissa", and from her nose to the end of her tail, she measured about seventy-five inches. Her tail alone was at least forty inches, and that twitching of it back and forth didn't do anything to help allay my fears. Her head, the one I faced at a distance of six inches, measured about a foot and a half.

All in all, it was a pretty terrifying experience, and one that had me shaking all the way to Arrowhead Springs, a good three-hour drive away.

I'm sure I wasn't the only one who suffered from acute fright that day. I bet there are any number of drivers who, years later, might still be wondering if they were seeing right. Seemed every time we stopped for a light—we didn't have freeways in those days—this animal would raise its head, look out the window, and snarl at the occupants of the next car. I've seen double-takes in my life, but none equal to the ones I saw that day!

I found out later that Olga Celeste had raised this particular leopard since it was a cub. In fact, she had raised it with a little fox terrier, and the two of them slept in the bed with her for the twenty years that the leopard lived.

At the time that I "met" Nissa, she was seventeen years old, and was a star of motion pictures. She co-starred with Katherine Hepburn and Cary Grant in "Bringing Up Baby". Some baby!

Olga told me later that in her entire career of training leopards, and she had trained plenty of them, she had come across only five of the animals that could be tamed in any way, and Nissa was the best of all of them. However, she did hasten to add that they were wild, and in her opinion, one that I found was shared by all wild animal trainers that I subsequently met, it is really impossible to tame them; they can only be trained. Maybe Olga had a special thing going for her, but personally, I could think of a more desirable bed companion.

The show was a huge success, but even the four hours we were there still found me shaking from my encounter with Olga's "pet".

I was determined not to ride back with that beast, so we changed station wagons for the ride back to town.

Whether that was the right decision still is a moot question because one of our companions was Chief Sugar Brown, head of a large family of Indians that came from some remote tribe in Oklahoma. The Chief was a weather-beaten old man, dressed in full regalia. Norman had trooped with the Sugar Browns on Russell Brothers Circus where they had performed in the Wild West Show, so he was pretty familiar with the Chief's habits. However, he neglected to tell me that the Chief's main hobby was singing war chants. All the way back to Los Angeles, the Chief chanted, beating out the rhythm on the door of the station wagon, while I sat appalled, expecting any moment that we would be scalped.

While I'm on the subject of those first experiences, I should relate another encounter with an animal. Just a few weeks after our marriage, we decided to drive over to the Seelig Zoo with Norman's friend, Harry Hammond, to see Mr. and Mrs. Delbert Graham, a couple that they had trouped with on Russell Brothers Circus.

They were wintering there in a trailer, and Norm had told me about their fantastic chimpanzee named Andy Colino, and he was anxious for me to see him.

My knowledge of any kind of primates was about as great as my knowledge of leopards, so I was really unprepared for what I was about to see. As we approached the entrance to the zoo, we could see a line of cars silently driving by what looked to me like a large monkey on a chain.

From the distance, the animal seemed completely oblivious to all the attention it was receiving, but as we entered the gates of the zoo, the silence that had pervaded was suddenly shattered. We were still a distance away from the Graham's trailer, but we could hear the unmistakable sounds that chimps make, a cross between a whoop and a grunt. To my uninitiated ears, it didn't sound a bit friendly.

As we approached the animal, the whooping became more insistent, and it wasn't until we stopped in front of the trailer and

Norman got out and went up to greet the chimp that all the commotion stopped.

Mrs. Graham came running out of the the trailer to welcome us, but she wasn't a bit surprised to see Norman, she said, because he was the only one who evoked such a reception from Andy Colino. Why, she didn't know, but she thought it was because Norman had always treated him with dignity in the circus.

Mrs. Graham graciously invited us into the trailer for coffee. She untied Andy, who was completely dressed in a shirt & overalls, and he ran ahead to open the door of the trailer for us. I'm sure I must have looked like an idiot with my mouth wide open as I watched this tremendous chimp,who was at least five feet tall and weighed 170 pounds, help Mrs. Graham set the table.

Joining us at the table he politely laid his napkin across his lap and waited until Mrs. Graham gave him a signal that it was all right to start eating his cake and drinking his Cola. I can truthfully say that he had better manners than many children I've seen.

After we finished the little snack, he cleared the table with all the proficiency of a well-trained maid. Mrs. Graham washed the dishes while Andy dried and put them away.

I was torn between complete wonder and not a little bit of fear because I had heard that chimps, especially large ones, were extremely dangerous. Evidently Andy had never heard about it because, according to a later conversation with Mrs. Graham, there was never a time in the seventeen years that she owned him that he didn't have a sweet disposition.

The only thing that disturbed him was to hear people fight or argue loudly. He would stamp his foot and start whooping, and she assured us that it was all it took to keep her household a peaceful one.

She had gotten Andy from Frank Buck, of "Bring 'em Back Alive" fame, when the chimp was a year and a half old and weighed 18 pounds. From that time, in addition to the training he received for the act in the circus, he lived with them as a member of the family.

He had his own bed, complete with sheets and blankets. He was toilet trained and took care of his own needs even to wiping himself. He always wore clothes and enjoyed having money in his pockets.

He was extremely affectionate, and if by chance Mrs. Graham should cry over something, he would wipe her tears away with a hanky, kiss her and generally try to comfort her.

When they got Andy, the Graham's grandson was about two years old, and he and Andy became bosom buddies. However, as they both got older, Andy would react rather violently to their scolding the little boy, and they decided it would be a better idea to keep them separated.

Andy seemed to sense pending events. Mrs. Graham cited the time before one of California's earthquakes when Andy's agitation alerted them to the danger. Perhaps that is why he was aware of Norman's arrival even though he couldn't have seen or smelled him as we entered the zoo.

As a rule, chimpanzees rely more on visual power than do other animals, and they depend less on olfactory. Structurally, man shares many characteristics with the chimpanzee. They are prone to many of the same diseases as man to which other animals are relatively immune. They also react to sedatives, stimulants and poisons the same as man.

The chimpanzee's marvelous imitative ability is what makes him such a delightful circus performer; and after seeing Andy Colino, it wouldn't have surprised me a bit to see some enterprising sharpy start training them to become domestic workers or ticket takers.

Don't think, however, that my short acquaintance with Andy made me discard caution where these animals are concerned. In the years I'd been with the circus, I've seen too many trainers without fingers and carrying any number of scars, to make me have a healthy respect for them, and to give them a very wide berth.

These experiences in the first days of our marriage should have prepared me for those to come, but I never ceased to be surprised.

CHAPTER FIVE

Our marriage was off to a bang-up start in more than one way. Two days after we were married, there was a knock on the door. I opened it, and there stood mother, bag and baggage. What had seemed to her to be an ideal living situation turned out to be a real bust, and naturally there was no place else for her to go but back to my apartment.

How our marriage managed to survive that little test, I'll never know because Norman had to move out and back to his mother's house until we found a new place for mama, and this little process took about a week. In the meantime, I saw my bridegroom about twice. Some honeymoon!

Eventually things simmered down, and as it was still off-season for the circus, Norman took on some odd jobs. One included doing some lifting which did the hernia no good, so I insisted that he had to have an operation.

The double hernia was a surprise to me on our wedding night. Even though we considered ourselves modern and enlightened, we hadn't slept together before marriage and a double hernia and a truss weren't high on my list of desirable attributes in a man. Reluctantly, he agreed to surgery and fortunately all went well.

By this time, we had been married about two months, and I was still working for Russian War Relief. During the time that Norman was recuperating from the operation, I was up to my ears in working on a concert at the Hollywood Bowl in which Joseph Zsgetti, the renowned violinist, would appear. The orchestra was under the direction of the famous conductor, Bruno Walter.

The day before the concert, which was a sell-out, there was a champagne cocktail party at the Beverly Wilshire Hotel. It was an unseasonably hot day and a hectic one. In fact, so hectic that I hadn't a chance to even have a cup of coffee. Normally this wouldn't have mattered, but at the reception I did take a glass of champagne, and in the excitement of meeting and greeting people, I didn't notice that every time I emptied the glass, a waiter would refill it. How many glasses of champagne I had drunk on an empty stomach, I'll never know.

Strangely enough, it didn't seem to bother me during the reception or on the taxi ride home, which I shared with one of the visiting committee members from San Diego.

In fact, I alighted from the cab across the street from our apartment and proceeded to walk across a thoroughfare that was as well-traveled as the freeways are now. All without incident. But when I opened the door to the apartment, WOW, all of a sudden the floor came up and hit me in the face, and I was never drunker in my entire life. Before or after!

Fortunately, that was the first day Norman could go out after the operation, and he had gone down to Hollywood Boulevard to meet his mother and brother, so he wasn't there to see his soused spouse.

Even in my drunken stupor, I had enough sense to realize that he might not appreciate my behavior, and I was determined to get undressed and into bed before he returned, thinking I could feign sleep , and he'd never know the difference.

Our one room apartment consisted of the living room, which contained a double studio couch, kitchen, dressing room and bath. I managed to make it to the dressing room and was struggling to get undressed when Norman walked in the front door.

I can only guess at his reaction when his inebriated wife peered sheepishly around the corner of the dressing room, hand up in front of my nose, beckoning him with one finger to come in.

Poor Norm, he was convinced he had married a lush. We hadn't known one another very well before we were married, and if there was anything that he couldn't tolerate, because his father had been an alcoholic, it was people who drank too much.

At this point, I was too drunk to stand up alone, and he was too weak to hold me up, but he did manage to get me to bed and started plying me with black coffee. He was torn between walking out and leaving me and feeling sorry for me because by this time I was deathly ill. The night seemed an eternity, and then the morning came altogether too soon. I had to be at the Hollywood Bowl at eight a.m.

A champagne hangover is unlike any other. If you take a sip of water, you're drunk all over again, and if you look down, the sidewalk comes up and hits you right in the eye.

When Norm saw how miserable I was, I guess he decided to forgive me, feeling I had been punished enough. Actually, the punishment was just starting, and how I ever made it up to the top of the Bowl to check the sound, I'll never know.

That was a day to remember, and I certainly have. It's a rare occasion when I'll take a drink of champagne, and then it's only one.

CHAPTER SIX

I'd like to say that we settled down to a quiet married life, but in the twenty-two years of our marriage, I can truthfully say it was anything but quiet, and most certainly it was never dull.

After the leopard episode, I should have been prepared for anything, but as I said, I was naive. Russell Brothers-Pan Pacific Circus, owned by Art Concello, was going to open in all its tented glory on the Pan Pacific parking lot in Los Angeles, and Norman was the announcer and ringmaster, and was also the talker on the side show.

Some of the circus performers started to arrive in town prior to the opening, and it was only natural that they call Norman. Being a warm, hospitable man, he promptly invited them over for lunch or dinner and to meet his new bride.

The first invitation was extended to Margaret Ann Robinson and her mother to join us for lunch. I went all out in setting the table, using our best silverware. Naturally, I was anxious to make a good impression on his friends. There was only one thing; my dear husband had neglected to tell me anything about Margaret Ann.

All I knew about her was that she worked in the side show. When the doorbell rang, I answered it, hand extended in welcome, eyes straight ahead. To my surprise I was looking into thin air! Only then did I glance down, and there, standing all of about 24 inches from the floor, was Margaret Ann Robinson.

Margaret Ann's mother, a normal-sized woman, was standing on the stairs, and that was why I didn't see her first. You can imagine my surprise. Like everything else I was coming in contact with, this was a first for me. Of course, I had seen the famous Singer Midgets in vaudeville when I was a little girl, but I had never seen one up close.

All our plans for an elegant table had to go out the window. For one thing, when Margaret Ann sat on a regular-sized chair she couldn't begin to reach the table. Consequently, every large book in the house had to be put to use. The silverware I had set the table with had to be discarded because a dinner fork in Margaret's hand was like a shovel. We substituted a pickle fork and managed to make it through lunch.

Margaret Ann was exceptionally tiny, even for a midget. At the time I met her she was in her early twenties. Born of normal parents with a normal-sized younger sister, Margaret Ann, like most midgets, was normal at birth and for several years thereafter.

Midgets are the victims of malfunctioning glands, among which the thyroid and pituitary are the chief offenders. The pituitary dominates the thyroid, yet works in close partnership with it. They share the burden of bone growth, but whereas the thyroid is chiefly concerned with the leg, arm and head bones, the pituitary most actively affects those of the torso. Both too, dictate phases of sexual capacity and capability.

Scientists have placed midgets in three classifications, but they all look alike to the layman. All are alike in appearance. Two of the classifications are alike in every particular except the matter of birth and growth. The third is totally different from the other two except in the matter of size.

The three classifications are: (1) an infantile midget; (2) a primordial midget; (3) a true midget. Infantile midgets have no sexual capacity beyond that of a baby, however, intelligence is normal. Like true midgets, their bone ends never close; thus, they could grow at anytime during their lifetime. Primordial midgets are characterized by the fact that dwarfism exists already at birth; apart from the smallness, the development proceeds normally. Their bone ends close in their early twenties, just as with normal individuals, and their sexual development also parallels the normal.

True midgets are normal-born children of normal parents. The stoppage of body growth, which means "midgetdom", may occur at any time from infancy to the immediate preadolescent years. Sexual development is normal, consistent with size. Sexual capability is normal, and sexual capacity, although sometimes somewhat limited, also is normal. However, a sexual potency seldom develops before the very late teens or early twenties. True midgets form the vast majority of the world's midget population.

It is disturbing to note that any man or woman capable of begetting children may be the parents of midgets. Perhaps more disturbing to contemplate is the fact that infants and small children in apparently normal health have no guarantee against "midgetism". Let me hasten to add, however, that the odds against midgetism are placed at a million to one, and science has come a long way since some of these statistics were written.

The average layman is apt to confuse a midget and a dwarf, thinking that all abnormally small people are alike. Actually, midgets can best be described as perfectly proportioned little people who are a miniature copy of ourselves. Dwarfs, on the other hand, have a normal-sized, scanty-haired trunk, topped by a disproportionately large head. The face is the shape of an inverted pear, with the nose saddle-shaped and broad at the root and bridge. The arms are short and carried away from the body. The lower limbs are short and massive and misshapen; hands and feet are short, thick and broad, and the fingers are of equal length, as are the toes. Both men and women have excessive muscular development. The intelligence is usually normal, as is the voice.

They are primarily the victims of an under-functioning thyroid. Some or most of the other glands may be involved—science is still in the process of determining this—but the thyroid is the tyrant in the dwarf's case. The thyroid does not provide sufficient thyroxine so that the dwarf's arms and legs are shortened and malformed, and his head grotesque. On the other hand, his thoroughly alert pituitary provides a normal flow of sex hormones, and his normal sexual capacity, and his sexual organs are as large as those of normal individuals. His pituitary also manufactures sufficient growth hormones to equip him with a normal torso.

Midgets tend to consider dwarfs minor monstrosities, almost a race apart from themselves, and they bitterly resent being called or considered dwarfs. Toward these little people of fantastic form, they hold a smug attitude very similar to that held by normal-sized people toward them.

A classical example was when Norman took little Felix Silla, a very small but normal midget, to look for an apartment in Hollywood where he was working in movies. They found several that were perfect for his needs but when the landlords found out they weren't for Norman but for Felix, they refused to rent to a midget. Fortunately, we found out about a small hotel that catered to the "little people", and Felix not only got his apartment but a whole circle of new friends. For that matter, we really became the beneficiaries because the little people became our dear friends and used to call us the world's tallest midgets.

All this may digress from our luncheon that day, but I know that I was completely in the dark regarding the "little people" as they prefer to be called, until I really delved into the subject, and I would hope that the foregoing information might prove illuminating. I feel honored that I had many dear little friends, and I hope I was always worthy of their friendship.

While on the subject of "little people", this might be the appropriate time to tell about another experience that happened shortly after we were married. Norman was very fond of a little dwarf clown named Alvah Evans. Alvah visited us several times, and we would see him in the circus, and when he was on tour, he would write us letters.

One day the good news came that Alvah had gotten married, and his letters were filled with glowing reports about his new bride. According to Alvah, she was not only beautiful, but she was very creative and wrote wonderful poetry. He was anxious for us to meet her, and as the circus season was coming to a close, they would be appearing in a side show during the winter on the old Long Beach Pike. So, would we come down to meet Lavonda? By all means, we were delighted.

The day arrived, and it was an extremely hot one, especially for wintertime. Alvah was waiting for us at the entrance to the side show which was in a large store. Excitedly he took us to meet his new wife. All I can say is that when I saw her, I turned as white as a ghost, and discreetly motioned to Norman to get me out of there because I felt I was going to faint. I'm certainly not the fainting type. In fact, I don't ever remember fainting, but if I hadn't gotten out of that building, I know I would have sprawled, all five feet nine inches of me, on the floor.

What I remember seeing was a full size head on what seemed to be a platter! Actually, Lavonda did have what passed for a torso, but it was folded under in such a way that you only saw her from just under the breasts up. Her arms were extremely thin and spindly and seemed to be at odd angles, and she wore a hearing aid.

At the time, she was in her thirties, and turned out to be a very nice person. I'm still inclined to think it was the heat that day that made me feel faint because I never had that reaction again. Or maybe it's just that when we become familiar with something, be it a person or an idea, it no longer seems odd or unusual to us.

Lavonda had to be carried, and Alvah seemed to enjoy the task. Her mode of transportation was a baby buggy, and one time on the circus, I even took a turn at wheeling her around.

Several years after she and Alvah were married, she made medical history, astounding doctors by becoming pregnant. They had to take the baby, but they were able to save her. Just how this miracle of pregnancy came about is still a mystery.

CHAPTER SEVEN

Russell Brothers-Pan Pacific Circus opened in 1945 at the Pan Pacific Auditorium in Los Angeles. Art Concello had bought Russell Brothers Circus and turned it into a railroad show and changed the title.

For a show of its size, it was a truly beautiful circus. The aerial ballet was designed by Norman Bel Geddes, and the acts were some of the finest in circusdom. It was a far cry from my last visit to the circus where everything seemed worn out and old. While all the equipment and props for this show were not new, everything had been freshly painted, and the whole circus sparkled.

Frank Buck, of the legendary "Bring Them Back Alive" fame was one of the big features. He rode into the tent on a "Howdah" atop a huge elephant and waved greetings to the audience. Unfortunately, at one of the performances, someone let the lions into their caged arena before their time and his elephant freaked! Poor, "brave" Frank Buck was holding on for dear life screaming, "Get me off this damn thing!"

I was meeting some of the aristocracy of the circus for the first time, and I was most impressed. Circus performers were unlike any other show people I had ever met. It's almost as if they lived in a world apart, and it's a clannish world, or at least it still was at that time. Now, it is a little different.

They were extremely religious people and very family-oriented. While they may have their moments, for the most part they lived very clean, wholesome lives. This isn't too hard to understand when you realize that for many, their very lives depended upon their alertness and coordination.

It is only in the United States that the average person is inclined to think of circus people as itinerant gypsies. In Europe, circus performers are accorded with the same kind of adulation that opera stars receive. European circuses are quite different from ours in that they are one-ring affairs. Also, the pace is completely different. It is a slow pace, wherein the performers have the opportunity to really display their particular skills.

Here, we are so attuned to speed and the confusion of many things taking place at the same time that we do not give much thought to the individual performer. We also have the tendency to lump circuses and carnivals together. They couldn't be farther apart. It is like comparing opera and burlesque, and circus performers become highly insulted at the comparison.

In the past (and to a certain extent, it still exists especially in some of the smaller shows), there had been a real caste system in the circus. This was apparent in the cookhouse or cook tent. This was the low tent in the "backyard" of the circus that served, or in some of the smaller shows, still may serve as the dining room of the circus.

When the flag was up, the signal that the meal was being served, performers entered one side of the tent and working men, the other. The sides were separated by a canvas wall with the performers' side called the "short-side" and the working men's, the "long-side".

The performers' side usually had red checked tablecloths, and the working men's had either blue or none. The food was the same for both sides; however, the dishes and utensils may have differed. On the performers' side the tables were assigned at the beginning of the season on the basis of so-called rank. The choice tables going first to the top brass and front office staff; then came the aristocrats of the circus, the aerialists, then acrobats. There was a single girls' table, a clown table, side-show table, and others; it was considered bad taste to sit at any other place than where you were assigned.

Perhaps this rather strange background helps contribute to the fact that circus people may seem different from those in other branches of show business.

Strangers are not readily accepted into their world, but Norman was extremely popular with everyone in the circus—from the lowliest, the man who put up the donikers (or toilets), to the circus owners—and I was warmly welcomed.

I remember that practically all of the performers would come up to me and tell me what a great announcer Norman was, and I thought they were just being kind because up to that time, I hadn't heard him either in the Big Show or on the Side Show. When I did, I knew that it wasn't just kindness; he really was the greatest outdoor show announcer that the circus had ever known. His voice was so powerful that once, when the sound went out in the Los Angeles Coliseum during a revival showing of the 101 Wild West Show, he could be heard in every corner without the aid of a microphone.

The circus was doing a fantastic business. These were the war years, before television, and the circus, the perennial purveyor of fun for children of all ages, was bringing a little respite from the worries of war, taxes and rationing.

Then one day, some days after the circus opened, came the world-shaking news that President Franklin Delano Roosevelt had passed away. Everything came to a stop; performances were canceled, and the people seemed to be in a state of shock. When the show resumed, business dropped and never did pick up for the remainder of the Los Angeles engagement.

All this time, my knowledge of the circus was still pretty cursory. I was still working and had very little time to go around the show, and when I did, it was always with Norman.

It wasn't until the fall of that year that the team of "The Carrolls" came into being. Cole Brothers Circus was coming to town, and Zack Terrell, the venerable owner, contacted Norman about the possibility, with my contacts, of staging a real Hollywood opening for the event and handling radio publicity. I could help with getting the motion picture stars, and we proceeded to turn our one-room apartment into an office.

We had no experience doing radio publicity but as the old saying goes, "fools rush in where angels fear to tread", and we dived in with both feet and managed to pull off a successful campaign. Our efforts produced a bang-up premiere, and the carry-over resulted in the show doing record business.

It didn't take long for word to go through the circus grapevine that if a show was planning on playing Los Angeles, it might be a good idea to contact The Carrolls, and thus we were launched into the publicity business.

In the meantime, I was learning more and more about the circus, but it was still an unknown quantity as far as I was concerned. Of course, I was never around the circus without Norman, so it wasn't too important that I didn't know the inner workings of a circus.

In 1946 Norman joined the Clyde Beatty Circus. This was the Russell Brothers-Pan Pacific Railroad Show, now sold to Clyde Beatty by Art Concello. When it played Los Angeles, we were both signed to handle publicity (thus I became the first woman circus press agent) and we continued to do so for the entire lifetime of the circus—until a series of mishaps, disastrous weather and a strike caused it to fold in 1956.

Clyde Beatty was undoubtedly one of the greatest wild animal trainers to have ever lived. He was not the first man to have ever mixed male and female lions and tigers in one arena, but he was the first to do it on a large scale. At one time, his huge steel cage held forty lions and tigers. I didn't know Clyde Beatty in those days, but I can assure you I was plenty impressed by the twenty-some he was working when I first saw him.

A small, muscular, wiry man, Beatty had been around wild animals since 1919 when, as a circus-happy kid, he had run away from his home in Ohio to join Howe's Greater London Circus. I don't know what compulsion motivates people to take up dangerous professions like wild animal training, but I do know that there seemed to be an unnatural communion between him and his animals. In fact, many times I felt that he and his handsome tigers bore a strong resemblance to each other.

He used only jungle-bred animals in his act, feeling that a captivity-bred animal, that may have been pampered and indulged as a young cat, became a sullen and unmanageable adult.

Of all the modern wild-animal trainers, Clyde Beatty presented the purest version of the All—American "fighting act". This type of act displays the beasts as dangerous jungle killers as opposed to the European tendency of presenting a "still act" where the animals are presented in posed tableaux, and the trainer works them in a calm manner that would indicate complete control.

While the European acts are fascinating to watch, I have always felt that they lacked the thrill of the "fighting act". When Beatty entered the arena, armed only with a chair and a whip, there was always an audible murmur of anticipation and excitement that could be heard throughout the audience.

It's true that Beatty had a gun, and used it frequently, but it was just for effect and contained only blanks. The average layman doesn't realize that if he were to have had real bullets in the gun and did try to shoot an animal, it could have resulted in a real disaster if the bullet either missed its mark or were to just graze the cat.

Beatty always considered the sturdy, four-pronged chair his best protector, giving the cat something to chew on instead of the trainer. The whip and pole were used mainly for cueing the animals.

It was always a constant source of amazement to me that Clyde did not consider his profession to be unusual. A perfect example of this was one night when he managed to talk Norman and me into attending the prize fights at the old Hollywood Legion Stadium. Clyde loved the fights, and it was only his persuasiveness that made me agree to go. I had never been to the fights, and I had no desire to go, but I felt I had to be a good sport.

It happened that the main event was a pretty gory affair with both fighters bloody and battered. Clyde, who had just been clawed by one of his lions and was still sporting bandages, was sitting on the edge of his chair. When the final blow was struck which sent one of the fighters crashing to the floor, Clyde leaned over to me and said, "Gee, Shirley, can you imagine anyone wanting to make a living that way?"

CHAPTER EIGHT

The spring of 1948 brought some big changes to our lives. Norman was offered the job of assistant director of radio publicity on Ringling Brothers and Barnum & Bailey Circus, and he was also to be the Big Show announcer for the evening performance.

This was the realization of his dream. To the circus performer, in those days, a season on the Big One was the equivalent of a vaudeville performer being signed to play the "Palace". It was too good an offer for him to turn down in spite of the fact that we were signed to handle the publicity for the spring opening of the Clyde Beatty Circus in Los Angeles. The only solution was that I would have to go it alone on the Beatty Show after Norman helped set up the campaign.

By this time, I had become rather accomplished in radio publicity, but that wasn't the part that worried me; it was, that I really didn't know my way around the circus too well without Norm. He assured me that I would learn, and that all would be OK.

Parting was sweet sorrow in more than one way. First, we had only been married three years and I didn't enjoy the idea of being separated, and second, I was scared silly at the prospect of what awaited me at the circus. The campaign was a huge success, and never in the history of circuses playing Los Angeles had anyone seen anything to equal the business of this engagement.

We did four shows a day on the weekends and three shows a day during the week. The crowds were lined up for two blocks waiting to buy tickets. The campaign was warmly praised by Clyde Beatty, and everyone on the show, and naturally, I was pleased that I hadn't let Norman down and that his confidence in my ability to carry on was justified.

The work, however wasn't my problem that year; it was my

ignorance that was showing that caused me to have a few bad moments. My favorite people in the circus at the time, were the clowns. And of that group, Bobby Kay, who later became one of the featured clowns with Ringling Brothers and Barnum & Bailey Circus, was my very favorite. Not only did I like him as a clown, he was my friend and my mentor. Without his subtle suggestions, when I committed a boo-boo, I'm sure I would have never made it. Of course, he wasn't always around to save me, but he did on more than one occasion.

The first time was in the cookhouse. You may remember my telling about the "caste" system. Until the day that I goofed, I wasn't aware of the rules, and so the first time I decided to eat in the cookhouse alone, I went directly to the clown table to be with my friends.

Circus people are extremely well-mannered and wouldn't for the world think of hurting anyone's feelings, so consequently nothing was said during the meal. It was only natural that I was self-conscious, and I thought that maybe I was just imagining all the raised eyebrows.

It wasn't until we had left the tent, and Bobby and I were walking alone across the backyard of the circus, that he tactfully told me that it just wasn't being done for anyone from the staff to sit with the clowns, or for that matter any place but at the staff table. When I protested that I didn't know anyone there too well, he said the circus code of ethics didn't leave much latitude, and I had better start getting acquainted!

I'm convinced that my hair started turning gray with that engagement of the circus. I had always been in awe of elephants, but my acquaintance with them was a nodding one. I was well-versed in some statistics about them such as—they are all called "bulls", even though the majority of circus elephants are female; they have a life span equivalent to a human being, and some bulls have been known to reach 130 years in captivity.

They eat about 125 pounds of hay daily, 18 to 20 pounds of grain, plenty of pure dirt and all the peanuts they can cadge from the kiddies; they drink up to 25 gallons of water a day. They are subject to all the ills that we are, and in proportion to their size, they are covered with stiff, black hair that is like fine wire to the touch, and they have to be "shaved" with a blow torch; and they really have a lousy memory in spite of what people think.

But what I didn't know was that when you used elephants for publicity stunts, there were certain precautions to be taken that were very, very necessary unless you were anxious to meet an early grave.

I had arranged to take an elephant out to the CBS studios on Sunset Boulevard for an audience participation radio show called "Meet the Missus". The stunt was to see if an elephant really did have a good memory. This was a popular coast-to-coast show at the time, and it was a real *coup* to have the circus plugged on it.

So far, so good; only no one had bothered to tell me that I had to have a door high enough and wide enough for an elephant to get through, and it so happened that this show did not emanate from the main studios; it came from a converted warehouse down the street.

I rode out in the truck from the circus grounds with Whitey, the trainer, and Babe, the elephant. When we got to the studios, we found that the only door wide enough for Babe was on the side through what had been a loading dock. That wasn't so bad, but it wasn't tall enough for her, and the only way she could get through would be down on her knees!

Whitey assured me that it could be done, albeit with some difficulty, and then we discovered that once through the doors, it would be necessary for Babe to crawl through a store room to get to the stage of the studio. With my aging by the second and Whitey gently coaxing Babe, we made it, only to have Whitey ask me when we reached the door to the stage whether it was reinforced enough to hold a five-ton elephant! Frankly, I was sure it wasn't because I felt like I had just fallen through it!

No one seemed to know the answer to that little question, and we decided to take our chances. All through the show, I had visions of Babe falling through the floor or taking off through the audience of several hundred people. But thanks to a sponsor whose main product was peanuts, we fed that poor beast peanuts by the pound, box and all, and fortunately Babe behaved like a lady through the whole messy bit.

My initiation into the circus was now complete; I could make guest appearances on radio, when the actual performers were not available, and pretend to be an aerialist, acrobat, equestrian and even an elephant trainer, and manage to sound authoritative. My husband had successfully taught me the valuable lesson of sounding enthusiastic, and it not only stood me in good stead that year, but it has continued to do so throughout the years.

It was a great engagement, but it couldn't end too soon for me. I was anxious to get to New York and to my darling. Outside of our writing and phoning, we kept in contact by trying to catch each other's plugs on various radio shows, because in reality, we were in competition with each other; and while it's great in business, it doesn't do a thing for a marriage!

He taught me another valuable lesson. At this time, the Clyde Beatty Circus owed us money and Clyde and Art Concello, who was the manager, were known for not being the greatest when it came to paying. Norman insisted I collect; but even though I towered above them—they were both short—I still didn't know how to approach them.

Finally, my clever husband came to the rescue by telling me to go to the "red wagon", the circus office that contained one desk and one chair and to be sure to sit down. It seems that psychologically, the fact that they now towered over me made them more amenable to my entreaty and sure enough, I walked away with every cent and my husband's admiration.

CHAPTER NINE

At this point, I should say a word or two about my dear husband and his reputation. True he was known throughout the circus world as the greatest announcer and side-show talker in the business and as one of the best publicity men in the outdoor show field, but he was also known as one of the most temperamental.

Norman was a perfectionist in his work, and he refused to settle for anything less; so consequently, it didn't take much for him to get on his high horse, and if things didn't work the way he felt they should, away he would go. In fact, it was said around the circus at that time, it took two people, one to say "Here he comes!", and another to say "There he goes!"

I can't remember at what point in the spring of 1949 he joined Cole Brothers Circus, which was now under new management, but I do remember that once again I was left in Los Angeles to do the Beatty show campaign. But this time the separation was going to be a short one. As soon as I finished with the circus, I would join Norman on the Cole show.

We were sure it would be for the entire season, so we decided to give up the little apartment. I stored some of our possessions, and with seven large, loaded suitcases, I took the train for Cincinnati, Ohio to join my better half.

The circus was playing across the river in Kentucky; and inasmuch as I had arrived in the afternoon, during show time, Norman couldn't meet me, but the circus management was kind enough to send the staff station wagon to take me to the circus train.

Norman - Houston Shrine Circus 1949

Shirley & friend "Babe"

Russell Bros. Circus 1944

Norman and his "girls"

Olga Celeste and my nemisis, "Nissa"

Most of the Escalante Family in front of their circus in May of 1945.

Clyde Beatty

Clyde Beatty Circus - 1948 Los Angeles

Shirley & Clowns - Clyde Beatty Circus 1948

Shirley & Norman Carroll
Clyde Beatty Circus 1951

Clyde Beatty Circus 1948. My friends in Clown Alley presented me with a beautiful briefcase. (L to R) Bobby Kay, Laurence Cross and Mark Anthony.

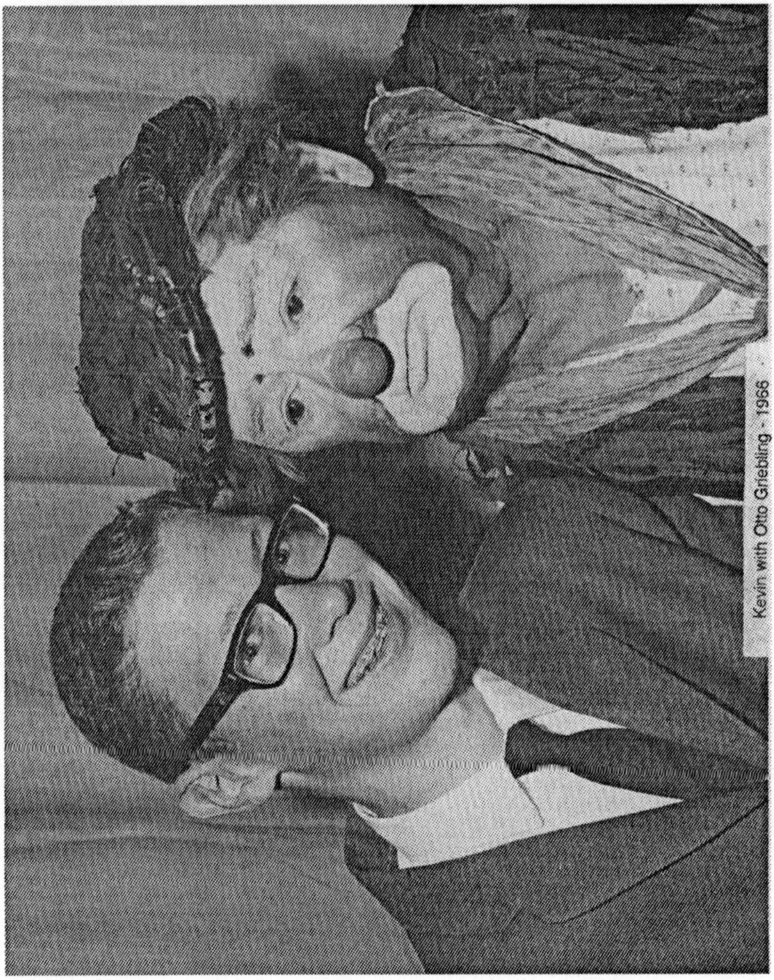

Kevin with Otto Griebling - 1966

The "little" people surprised me with a dinner party on my 48th birthday (l to r) Norman, Frank & Sadie Delfino, Harry Monte, Shirley, Kevin,Jerry Marren, Felix Silla & Harvey & Grace Williams.

Clyde Beatty Circus lion cub with Shirley & Kevin

Chuck Burnes & assistant "Kevin"

Now, it's true I had seen the Clyde Beatty Circus Train, and I had even eaten in the "pie" car, a special car that is set up as an "en route" lunch room and social center where performers congregate for coffee in the morning or a late snack at night; but I had never traveled on the train. Outside of visiting Clyde Beatty's private car, which was like a lovely five-room apartment, I had no idea what the living conditions aboard a circus train were like.

The station wagon stopped in some God-forsaken area, where the only touch of color was the bright, gaudily-painted train. I felt like an orphan in the wilderness until I heard a cheerful voice saying, "Welcome to your new home, Mrs. Carroll."

It was the porter assigned to our car, a tall cheerful man, nicknamed, "Yellow". Norman had asked him to take care of showing me around until he got there. His cheerful manner helped a little; that is, until he showed me to the stateroom that was to be my home for the next several months.

Our accommodations aboard the Cole Brothers Circus train were considered deluxe; and in fact, compared to some others I've since seen, they were. But at the first glance, our assigned quarters inside the train looked barely big enough for one person to even change their mind in, let alone big enough for two giants like us.

The stateroom was about six feet wide and about seven feet deep. It contained a double bed, set against the window, an inheritance from its previous occupant, and a real luxury. A small washbowl was in one corner and a closet on the other—taking up the remainder of the space between the bed and the door. All available space around the top of the entire stateroom was lined with cupboards.

I was still sitting on the bed trying to gather my wits about me when "Yellow" appeared with my luggage. Seven gigantic bags full of all kinds of unnecessary junk surrounded me, but it wasn't until Yellow closed the door, and the initial shock began to wear off, that the flood gates opened, and I started crying like a baby.

After about ten minutes of feeling very sorry for myself and ruing the day I had ever met Norman, I came to, and decided enough of this jazz; I had just better get with it and start turning a closet into a home. The next several hours were taken up with the pains-taking work of trying to make everything fit like sardines in a can; finally, I was ready to greet my husband.

Living on a train is unlike anything else in the world. Norman had neglected to tell me that all the cupboards must be locked before the train started to move. So naturally, the first night, after we were under way, something caused the train to stop with a resounding jerk, and the load of all seven suit cases came tumbling down on top of us. We were black and blue for days, but we were lucky we didn't get a concussion.

Then it took me ages to get used to the motion of the train and also the terrifying noise of a passing train letting go with their whistle just as our stateroom rolled by. The first few times this happened, I almost ended up on the ceiling, I was so scared. But time does wonders, and it even got to the point where, when we did play a town for several days and could go to a hotel, I found I had difficulty getting to sleep without the rocking motion of the train.

Another thing that took a little time to adjust to was the restroom facilities. This little room, which was dubbed the "honey bucket" by the performers, was shared by all the occupants of the car, and it was plenty odoriferous.

We were just fortunate we had a sink and running water; that is, we had running water when it was available, but there were plenty of times that we were stuck on a remote siding, and the water was cut off just when you were in the middle of brushing your teeth and still had a mouthful of toothpaste; or Norm would be in the middle of shaving and had a face full of lather.

The coach, a name applied on the circus to all sleepers, that we were assigned to, contained three staterooms that took up about one-third of the car; the other two-thirds held double berths.

Next to our stateroom was one occupied by a Chinese family, the Ming Sings. They were marvelous acrobats and contortionists, and I'm sure they had to be to all fit into that little room. The husband was Chinese, and the wife was Czechoslovakian, and they had two of the most adorable children I had ever seen. The other stateroom was the domain of the show's legal adjuster and his wife.

The berths were assigned mostly to married couples and to a few single men who were on the staff. Just as we could decorate our stateroom in any way that we wished, those in berths could decorate their little cubicles in any fashion that would spell "home" to them. So, it wasn't unusual to see anything from chintz curtains and bedspreads to bare blankets, depending on the imagination of the occupant.

Most of the other cars were similarly arranged, and the closeness of the setup didn't allow for much privacy. Everyone knew whether the married couples were getting along and who was sleeping with whom. In fact, the running gag around the show was that they would ring a bell at three in the morning, and everybody would go back to their own berths.

At night, after the show, it wasn't always convenient to go to the "pie car" for a snack because you were never sure if, out of the blue, the train would be divided and you would be stuck in the "pie car" while your car was miles or hours away. This happened to Norman more than one time, and it wasn't an unusual sight to see him hopping out of a cab in his pajamas and robe, trying to get "home".

We didn't have a regular stove, but we did the next best thing; we bought a little Sterno stove, and I proceeded to learn how to rough it. Funny, but those little snacks prepared on the "Rube Goldberg" contraption always tasted great.

More often than not, however, we would be treated to the exotic aromas of some delectable goody coming from our Chinese neighbors' room. Whereupon Norman and I would step out into the narrow passageway, donning our hungriest and leanest looks—which wasn't easy because at the time, we were just slightly smaller than a couple of elephants—until they took pity on us and would invite us to join them for a bite.

The husband did all the cooking and caring for the children while the wife just looked beautiful. I tried to talk Norm into that kind of arrangement, but he said the day I could do a back bend and pick up a glass of water with my teeth, we'd talk about it!

My experience with the train was traumatic. Now it was time to meet some of the top brass and the performers. I must say they were all cordial to this "first of May", the term give to newcomers who usually lasted for just one circus season.

One person who certainly stands out in my memory was "Barbette". He was the aerial and performance director who trained the girls for the "web" number. This is the rope the girls climb and then do all kinds of aerial acrobatics. Barbette was a dapper, slightly built, man who had been born in Paris, Texas and had once been the toast of the European Circus World. He performed as an aerialist on the single trapeze dressed as a girl. All the Royal Heads of countries where he appeared wined, dined and entertained him.

Some years before I met him, he had fallen from the trapeze and had broken every bone in his body, thus ending his performing career. He was now a gifted director (but a hard taskmaster) and a rather arrogant individual to most people.

Before I arrived on the show, he and Norman had hit it off, having several areas of interest in common—among them European culture. He was most gracious to me and remarked to Norman that he knew I was a lady because I always wore white gloves!"

Another outstanding memory of that season was meeting the Zacchini Family, famous for their Human Cannonball act. There were loads of Zacchinis out on various circuses with their cannons. The one we had on Cole Brothers Circus was headed by Hugo Zacchini.

In his early years, Hugo had studied painting in Paris and became intimately acquainted with the great artists, including Picasso. One day when we were discussing art, he said, "let me show you something", and took me over to the cannon whereupon he proceeded to extract a number of rolled up canvases. There were an original Picasso, Miro, Dali, and more, that had been given to him by the artists. When I realized these treasures were in the cannon, each time it was shot off I almost had a heart attack.

The Zacchini family drove the cannon from town to town and it created quite a stir in a community when shoppers at the local supermarket came upon the cannon in the parking lot!

It is a rarity for anyone to just go along for the ride on a circus, and while the press department on Cole Brothers didn't need any additional help, all my time wasn't entirely my own. I learned how to take tickets on the side show and to do other equally interesting if unchallenging tasks. But mainly, I would desert the hot, humid, dusty circus lot for the welcome air-conditioning of a hotel room.

I had struck up an acquaintance with the wife of the head concessionaire, and as this was also her first time out on a circus and we were both "first of Mays", we became close friends. She and her husband traveled by car and stayed in hotels and motels and were nice enough to invite me to visit anytime and to take a shower, a real luxury after our tiny sink.

In all, the tour was fun; I was seeing the country in an entirely different fashion than I had ever done before, and Norman and I were together. In fact, we were so determined to be together that we turned down an offer for me to come back to Los Angeles to handle radio and TV publicity for the Polack Brothers Circus.

I can't remember just what precipitated our leaving the show in Denver, but I do remember that tension had been building up, and when the manager heard that Norman was contemplating quitting, he threatened to hit him over the head with a stake. That was it! This time we had both had it, and I think it took us all of an hour to pack and be on a plane heading back to Los Angeles.

Actually, it was all quite an experience—one I wouldn't care to repeat—but one I'm grateful to have had.

CHAPTER TEN

We had given up our little $35 a month apartment, and now we had to go house-hunting. Inflation had really started with a vengeance, and the only thing we could find was a three-room unfurnished flat for $125 per month.

I was sure we would never be able to swing it, but Norman was the positive thinker in our family, and he assured me that all would be OK. Out of the blue, he received a call from a local television station, KTTV. They were initiating a new children's show, "Bozo's Circus", and they wanted Norm to be the announcer and ringmaster. It only paid $30 a week, which wasn't to be sneezed at but television was still a new medium at that time and compensation was minimal.

Also, we were personal representatives for Clyde Beatty, and Norman had come up with an idea for a "Clyde Beatty Radio show" which he consequently sold. Unfortunately, we were young and trusting, and what should have turned into a money-maker for all concerned, turned out to be a fiasco after the producers of the show decided that they had a good thing going and wanted all the profits. They managed to find a technicality in our letter of agreement, and we were out on our collective ears.

What they hadn't bargained for was the fact that the idea was Norm's, and he knew when, where, and how to develop it. Without him, it eventually fell apart, and everyone lost.

During the time that all was going well with the radio show, we were going great guns, what with the money we were getting from that and Norm's fling on TV. Like all good things, though, the TV show ended, and he decided to announce the Shrine winter date in Houston, Texas. Once again, I would have to hold down the home front because there were some picture deals for Clyde Beatty that Norman had been negotiating, and it was necessary to have someone available to answer any questions that might arise.

We had also made a commitment to the Hollywood Chamber of Commerce that the Clyde Beatty Circus elephants—all eight of them—would appear in the annual Santa Claus Lane Parade. It was my job to coordinate the circus' participation. Clyde was to ride in a "howdah", a seat on the back of an elephant, at the head of the parade, followed by a clown and show girls riding the other seven elephants.

At the time, the winter quarters of the circus was in El Monte, a town located about 30 miles east of Hollywood. I had made arrangements for the elephants to be trucked into town for the parade, and in all, it seemed to be a relatively simple matter.

The parade was to start just about six blocks from our apartment, so I decided it would be better to walk than drive and fight the traffic. My mother-in-law, who had never seen the Hollywood Parade, decided to spend the night with me, and though she was seventy years old at the time, she was extremely spry for her age; and the thought of the six-block walk didn't faze her. Beside, she was a good sport, and it was a real lark for her to be part of all the festivities.

So far, so good. We arrived ahead of the appointed hour at the assembly point for the parade, and in good time—so did Clyde Beatty, Bobby Kay, the clown, and the girls in their colorful, if somewhat scanty costumes.

Earlier in the afternoon, I had called winter quarters just to double-check and had been told that two trucks, with the elephants, had left at about 3:30 p.m., which would give them plenty of time before the 7:30 p.m. call. The parade was to start at 8 p.m., and I was just being cautious in having them there about an half-hour early, but I didn't want anything to go wrong. Little did I know then how wrong it was going!

We were all in a gay, holiday mood when we first assembled, but as the minutes started ticking away, and no elephants were in sight, we began to get a little jittery. I can still see us all standing on the corner peering down Hollywood Boulevard, like a bunch of Indians looking for the approach of the cavalry.

The parade officials were getting more panicky by the second, and so were we, but for different reasons. Elephants happen to be very valuable animals, and the eight that we were concerned about were highly trained, thus increasing their value by quite a few thousand dollars. Even in those days, they were worth at least $10,000 apiece.

Two more calls to winter quarters assured me that the elephant convoy had left there as scheduled, and that they should be arriving any second. We didn't have freeways in those days, and it took considerably longer to make the trip then, but still, it didn't take four hours! The thought of losing eight elephants in a cosmopolitan city was ludicrous, but still no elephants!

Now all I could envision was that the elephants had overpowered their trainers and had taken to the hills of Hollywood with their tails and trunks straight out in the air, trumpeting wildly and trampling everything in their way. Although, as upset as I was somehow the solution must be a simple one.

I thought that maybe the drivers had become confused and unloaded them on Sunset Boulevard instead of Hollywood Boulevard. With my mother-in-law running to keep up with me, we hot-footed the two blocks down to Sunset only to find no elephants. Maybe while we were gone, they had arrived, so back up to Hollywood Boulevard with my poor panting mother-in-law.

I was practically on a first-name basis with every motorcycle policeman in Hollywood by now, as I had them combing the side streets and alerting other units to be on the lookout for eight stray elephants. Imagine anything as embarrassing as losing eight elephants. Gloves, yes; hats, yes; umbrellas, yes; even dogs and cats; but elephants, forget it! (Although, Norman once lost his mother when he had taken her to visit a friend at the beach, and forgot where he left her!)

But that was exactly the situation when it was time to start the parade. They had held it up as long as possible for us; and we had reached the point of no return, so it had to start without Clyde and his beasts.

We were despairing of ever hearing of the elephants again; it was almost as if the earth had swallowed them up, when in the distance, coming down Hollywood Boulevard from the east, we heard the unmistakable trumpeting of our bulls. Sure enough, just as the last units of the parade were about to get into line, here came our foot-weary beasts and their block-headed keepers.

It seems they had misread the instructions and had unloaded the elephants in an empty lot on Hollywood Boulevard about three miles east of the proper location. True, they had arrived there early, at about 6 p.m., and the keepers figured that the reason they weren't seeing any activity was because it was too early. It wasn't until 8 p.m. that they finally began to suspect that maybe they had made a mistake. So, in tail-to-trunk formation, they started walking down Hollywood Boulevard in the hope of finding us.

We were so relieved that all we could do was to load Clyde, the clown and girls aboard and have them bring up at the rear of the parade, while mother O'Connor and I ran down to Sunset Boulevard to await them at the end of the four-mile long route.

It was a pretty sad sight. Eight pooped pachyderms and eight even more pooped handlers. One couldn't help being reminded of the tag line of a popular joke—"And give up show business"!

CHAPTER ELEVEN

The spring of 1950 found us pulling up stakes once again. We put our furniture in storage, and after the publicity campaign for the Clyde Beatty Circus was over in the Los Angeles area, we went ahead of the show as advance publicity agents.

The circus furnished us with a station wagon, and into this we loaded our necessary possessions and our portable office. We were ready for any eventuality, or so we thought. We learned the hard way that when we stayed in motels to ask for rooms off the highway; otherwise, like after our first night in Oxnard, it would seem that the trucks traveling the highway were coming right through our room.

In addition to the publicity chores we had, it was to be my job to "close schools". The idea being that I was to appear before the principals or school boards and be so convincing that they would have it no other way than for schools to be let out early so the children could attend the circus, and even more; they were to distribute discount tickets to the youngsters.

The theory was great. In the days before television, what could be more exciting to a youngster than a real, live circus? The only difficulty was that in the State of California, it was illegal to close schools for any other than state-authorized holidays. No one had told me about this rule, and like a fool, I ran where angels feared to tread. What's more, I was lucky. I did manage to get schools closed quite a number of times because apparently those in charge of the people I dealt with didn't know any more than I did. By the time I found out it couldn't legitimately be done, we were at the end of the school year, and I had to come up with a new gimmick to reach the small fry.

My husband was a great believer in "doing it yourself", and he refused to offer any suggestions, feeling that my rather limited brain needed the exercise. Of course, I would accuse him of not knowing, but I know now that his real concern was that I did learn to make use of my own abilities and not depend entirely on him. As it turned out, he was so very right. Plus the fact, he had made his living, most of his life, talking; and those long jumps between towns up north, meant a 125-mile long lecture, so it didn't take me long to come up with another idea.

About the only place where children congregated in that territory, during the summer, were the public libraries. They weren't as easy to convince as some of the schools, but eventually I managed to evolve an appealing program, and we were "in like Flynn" in every town.

The season found us going as far north as Seattle. It was late summer when we received word from Hollywood that the picture deal for Clyde Beatty might now be culminated, so back we came, again to no apartment. It's amazing how little these things matter when one is relatively young, and is together with a loved one. We finally found a little unfurnished house, high up on a hill.

The picture deals were made, and everything seemed to be coming up roses, except for one thing. We had been married eight years, and while we were happy together, we lacked the one thing we both wanted most in this world, a baby.

A miscarriage in the beginning of 1952 was a tremendous blow to both of us, and we decided to forget our sorrow in work. Our little house had two bedrooms, and we proceeded to turn one into an office. This was a tremendous improvement for us over the one room where we had previously worked, slept and ate.

In addition to doing the publicity for the Clyde Beatty Circus, we had a few other shows from time to time, and I was working for about four months for the Institute of Aeronautical Sciences, having taken the place of a girl who was leaving to have a baby. Maybe, it was catching! We couldn't have cared less what the explanation might be; we were just thrilled to find that in spite of our misgivings about it ever occurring again, I was pregnant.

My only problem was that I had the kind of constitution that had a tendency to abort, and my doctor insisted that I give up working when I was in the fourth month. I'm sure my employers were delighted because up until that time, the doctor had me so sedated that I was more like a walking zombie than a human being. Even though I didn't look very pregnant, Norman and I promptly went shopping for maternity clothes, all of which, as it turned out, I never got to wear until the last few weeks of my pregnancy.

Because of the abortive tendency, my doctor, knowing how anxious we were to have this baby, and knowing our ages, decreed that I would have to be confined to the house—if not to bed. I was allowed to spend the days on the couch in the living room and to walk around the house a little, but if I dropped something, it had to stay on the floor because I wasn't allowed to bend over to pick it up. This seemed like little enough sacrifice for what we hoped would be a wonderful result. The sacrifice went even further, because Norman had to give up a good deal of work out of town to stay home and take care of me.

We couldn't afford to hire anyone. In fact, we were up to our ears in debt; so, it was sort of a vicious circle. Norm couldn't leave town for an announcing job because we couldn't afford help, and we couldn't afford help because he wasn't working.

The darndest part of it all was that I never felt better. So much so, that when I was in my sixth month I decided I simply couldn't stand the dirty windows one minute longer and I would wash them. Norm had gone to deliver a shower present for my predecessor at the Institute, and I was alone. No sooner had I finished one window than I knew something was wrong. I couldn't reach Norm, but I did manage to call my doctor, and he came rushing over. Those were the days when doctors did that sort of thing.

When he first arrived, there were quite a few bad moments when he thought he might not be able to save the baby. Fortunately for us, my doctor was a brilliant man who came from Germany, and he was not only a fantastic obstetrician, but he was one of the kindest and most concerned men I had ever met. Thanks to his knowledge, medication, concern and plenty of prayer, I was OK. In fact, his concern was so great that from then on, I was confined to bed until he was assured I was well into my ninth month.

The baby was due in the middle of January, and it wasn't until New Year's Day that the doctor finally decided I could get up and that it would be all right for me to do all the things that had been pending. Little things like turning an office into a nursery, buying all the furniture and getting a layette together.

By this time, I was so "stir crazy" that getting out of the house was a real delight. Outside of watching TV, my only recreation for months had been lying on my back, not contemplating my navel, but watching the baby kick. I was sure it would be a boy, and I was also sure he would be born riding a bicycle!

Another thing, time was flying and there was so much to be done. Norman had received a wonderful offer from Ringling Brothers Circus. He was to be the Director of Radio and TV publicity, and it was necessary for him to get down to winter quarters as soon as possible. I would be doing the Clyde Beatty Circus campaign alone again, but by now that was old hat, so it wasn't a problem. Our only problem was that the time came for the baby to be born, and no sign of a baby.

By the end of the month we were both ready to tear our hair out. Norm simply had to leave early in February, and this time he couldn't turn down the offer because by now we were about $5,000 in debt, a tremendous sum in those days. For us, a baby didn't come cheap!

I carried groceries, walked up and down stairs and did everything within reason that I hoped would hasten the advent of our heir. No luck. For one who didn't dare take a really deep breath for fear of aborting, this was some switch.

Every night I would go into the nursery, look at the darling crib and despair of ever seeing a baby in it. Finally on the very last day of January, the time did come! We had carefully rehearsed this momentous occasion. The bag had been packed for weeks, and we had assured each other we would be calm.

Instead, when I awakened Norm at about 5:30 a.m. our bedroom took on all the aspects of a Mack Sennett comedy. First of all, we couldn't find our glasses, and we were both blind as bats without them. Then, we couldn't find the bag, which if we had our glasses on we probably would have fallen over; then Norm couldn't find the keys to the car.

After what seemed to me to be an eternity, but was in fact just a short time, we got to the hospital. I was sent to labor room number four, and Norman was sent home to await a call from the doctor. There was a phone in the room, and Norman called me every half hour. I think in the other half hour, he went out and watered the lawn until, in desperation, our landlady told him if he didn't stop watering the lawn, she would ask us to move because she was sure he had already drowned it.

I had gone into the hospital at 6:30 in the morning, and at 7:42 p.m. that Saturday night, our son, Kevin Carroll O'Connor was born. He weighed eight pounds, four ounces, and was 21" long; and I thought he was the most beautiful baby in the world.

Norman was beside himself with joy. I can still remember him coming to my bedside after he had been shown his son, and I had the distinct impression that he had floated into the room instead of walking in. Never had there been a baby more wanted, and never were there two happier parents.

We brought Kevin home on the fifth day, and the nurse we had hired greeted us at the door, but Norm wouldn't let her carry the baby for fear she would drop him. Having grown up in a family of thirteen, where there were always new babies, he was completely at ease with the new arrival; whereas, I was scared silly. I had never been around babies, and when Kevin cried, it practically sent me into hysterics. Fortunately for me, he was a good baby, once we found the right formula, and didn't do too much crying.

We were a little nutty where the baby was concerned, and I had the nurse washing down the entire nursery every day with Lysol. Visitors, including our families, hardly got a good glimpse of him because we didn't want anyone to breathe near him. I even made my darling mother-in-law wear a mask. It still is amazing to me that he managed to survive our over-solicitous care.

Messages of congratulations and gifts poured in from all our circus friends, and it isn't every baby that can boast of having received a darling red toy pony from the tattooed lady and the armless boy. Both wonderful people.

Now our life was a four-ring circus, and the only thing that marred our happiness was the prospect of Norman leaving for the east. I promised to take pictures often and to keep him minutely informed regarding Kevin's growth and development.

I had some traveling to do, so we decided to keep the nurse until I had finished the Beatty Circus campaign. Outside of bottle feeding Kevin, I didn't get to do many of the necessary chores for the baby. What I did do, was to follow our pediatrician's advice to "take him home and enjoy him." My only regret was that Norman wasn't sharing these precious first few months.

Finally, I was through with the Beatty Show and could devote all my time to my son. The nurse left us in the early part of May, and I was terrified. The first night I slept on the nurse's bed in the nursery for fear that I wouldn't hear him if he cried out in the night. I say "slept", but that's a misnomer because there wasn't any sleeping that night.

Until that night, I had no idea that little infants could make so much noise. The snorting and other assorted sounds were unbelievable coming from one so small, and it was after that debacle that I decided Kevin needed a rested mother more than an overly concerned, and I moved back to my own room.

While taking care of an infant isn't the most scintillating occupation in the world; for me, it was a delight to watch the many changes taking place each day. My only problem was that it was such a new physical experience for me that I never knew I had so many bones and muscles that could all hurt at the same time. It didn't take me long to decide that maybe the nursery didn't have to be washed with Lysol every day!

CHAPTER TWELVE

By the first of June, Norman could stand it no longer. He simply had to come home, and he left the show with the promise that he would pick it up for the western tour.

He had left Los Angeles when Kevin was ten days old and pretty tiny, and he returned to find a hefty infant who had already developed a distinct personality of his own. I'm sure the transition was a little difficult for him to take, mainly because he resented having lost out on all that first growth period. But it didn't take long for the two to get acquainted, and Norm was completely captivated.

Time flew by, and before we knew it, the Ringling Show was heading for Los Angeles, and we were up to our ears in the radio and TV campaign. One of the shows that we had set was Art Linkletter's Houseparty, and we had arranged to have a giant from the side show appear as a guest.

The circus was then playing in Long Beach, and we drove out to pick up the giant, a young Englishman about eight feet tall. At that time, our car was a two-door sedan, and while it took a little doing, we managed to get him in the back seat.

He was a very pleasant, literate chap, and he was intrigued with Kevin who was then about seven months old. He asked all kinds of questions about him, and then he wanted to know how much he had weighed at birth. When I told him what a big baby he was, he told me that he had weighed just about six pounds when he was born.

Giants are mentioned a half a dozen times in the Old Testament, and the ancient Jews were firm believers in the existence of races of giants. Most conspicuous of the giants of the Old Testament was Goliath who fell before little David's slingshot.

Just as we have seen that midgets are victims of the whim of the pituitary glands, so are the so-called giants. Giantism in humans results from an over-secretion in childhood of the growth hormone of the anterior lobe of the pituitary gland.

Usually, we see abnormally tall people with an excessive enlargement of the jaw, the hands, feet, nose, lips and a general overgrowth of the bones of the body. This condition is due to a swelling of the pituitary gland and is defined as acromegaly, and acromegaly is invariably associated with giantism.

Dr. Woods Hutchinson declared that he had found giants invariably sexually weak. He also found that few children are known to have been born to them, and of those few, all were of normal size. In most cases, he found, there is great strength in early youth, but this is short-lived and soon gives way to feebleness, and old age comes upon them in early life.

I haven't known that many giants to say that the above is a true statement, but the few I have known have been rather young men. In light of the number of basketball players we see today, some of Dr. Hutchinson's theories, especially when it comes to sexual activity, may be subject to question.

Our young giant friend was completely at ease during the long ride from Long Beach to Hollywood and seemed to be comfortable enough in the back seat. It wasn't until we arrived at the studio and attempted to get him out of the car that our troubles began. Evidently sitting in one posture for so long had caused some kind of muscle spasm, and the poor boy simply couldn't manage to maneuver himself into any kind of position that would allow him to get by the pushed forward front seat.

By this time, we had accumulated a large crowd of "experts" all trying to tell us how to extricate him. In the meantime, it was getting later and later, and the TV show time was fast upon us. None of the suggestions worked, and in desperation we called someone to come and take the front seat of the car apart. Only then did we manage to free our captive, who came out bent like a pretzel, thereby blowing the TV show because how could we show a giant doubled in half! Rest assured he rode back to the circus in the front seat!

The following spring found Norman deciding not to return to the east for the Ringling show but to handle it just in California. He felt life was just too short to be separated for so long from those you love, and as it turned out, he was so right.

We had plenty to do out here what with the spring opening of the Clyde Beatty Circus because we not only handled it for Los Angeles but for the outlying areas as well. Shortly before the circus was to open in L.A., I felt we simply had to have something visual to take on TV shows to stir up a little interest.

The circus was in the general vicinity, but with two shows a day, it just wasn't possible to be bringing in some of the circus stars for guest appearances. I had the brilliant idea that we should have an animal. Not just any animal, but one of the adorable lion cubs that had recently been born on the show. This was all well and good, but the problem of transporting it back and forth to the show was still there.

I was particularly taken with one cub, and to save the trips to the show, I talked Clyde into letting me keep the cub in our basement, much against Norman's better judgment. He had spent most of his life around animals of all kinds, and he had the kind of healthy respect for them that one acquires after such an association.

I just loved animals, period, and I couldn't see what was wrong with keeping this cute cub at home. He agreed to let me, but only on the condition that he would have nothing to do with it, and it was all my responsibility.

We kept him tied to a long leash, and I took him for walks much to the amazement and amusement of my neighbors. When I took him to TV shows, he sat in a box on the front seat of the car and seemed to enjoy looking out of the window—of course, getting the same kind of reaction from drivers as did my leopard friend.

Kevin was still a little baby, and it kept me hopping fixing formula for Kevin and the cub, but this was satisfying my latent desire to be an animal trainer.

The first few days were fun, and then the little devil seemed to get meaner by the day. He was OK with me, but he would have no part of any man, and when it was time to return him to the circus, I certainly wasn't a bit sorry. My animal training aspirations had certainly vanished.

I found out later that he had grown up to be a killer, and Clyde had to give him to a zoo. I've often wondered if his early experience with me as an over-anxious "mother" had anything to do with it!

That was the same season that I had a "bath by fire" on TV. Every year we had done the arrival of the circus on TV in some form or another, but this was the first year we were going to go all out.

The station was KTTV, and they had assigned their top men, Bill Welsh, John Rovick (Sheriff John) and George Putnam, to do the coverage. In the past, Norman had always handled this aspect of the promotion, and outside of the original setting up of the arrangements, I had nothing to do with it.

This particular morning Norman awakened with a raging fever, and it was impossible for him to even get out of bed, let alone go down to the railroad unloading area. So naturally, who else? I was elected.

The circus train was due to arrive at 7:30 a.m., and the pre-publicity attending the arrival had been tremendous. When I arrived at the location at 7 a.m., not only the crew from the TV station were there, but the railroad yards were jam-packed with people. The plan was to televise the arrival of the train and the unloading, and then move to the circus lot location at Washington and Hill streets, and catch the entire setting up of the circus.

In those early days of TV, time wasn't as precious as it is today, and programming was flexible, so it was possible to stay with an event, if it was interesting, for as long as necessary. We were all waiting for the train to arrive when word came that there was a delay, and it would be at least an hour late. With that, the crew and commentators decided to move another camera up to the lot at Washington and Hill, a distance of some four miles, and to leave me at the unloading area.

Prior to that, I had been on camera with one or another of the M.C.'s discussing various aspects of the circus, and now I was to carry on alone. It's true I had been on a circus train on the Cole show, but believe it or not, I had never seen a circus train unload! And here I was supposed to be an authority on the subject and convince thousands of people that I knew what I was talking about.

It was only my husband's lessons in enthusiasm that saved me. As it turned out, I was on the air for several hours doing everything from interviewing people who were standing around waiting for the train to arrive to talking about everything I had ever read (or written) or heard about the circus.

When the train did finally arrive, after what seemed to me to be an eternity, I proceeded to describe the unloading as though I knew what I was talking about, and people who had been watching it on TV later came up to me on the lot and complimented me for making it so interesting and also commenting that I must have seen the trains unloaded a number of times to sound so enthusiastic and authoritative.

By the time we did the unloading, and I arrived at the circus grounds, I was a wreck. At that point I didn't care if I ever saw another circus train or for that matter, a circus, ever again! I had been on camera for several hours straight. It did have its compensations though; I was offered a job on the station, thanks to my ability to *ad lib*.

All this while Norman was watching it at home, but not without a little circus of his own going on in the living room. It seems Kevin, who was then about fourteen months, was watching too; and when he saw his mommy in that little window, he started crying for mommy to pick him up. He couldn't understand why she didn't come out of there!

CHAPTER THIRTEEN

Kevin was growing into a fine youngster, and we were slowly managing to extricate ourselves from all the prenatal debts. We had taken on some new accounts that included the Livestock Show, the Dairy Show and Jungleland; or as Norman put it, "We play the manure circuit!" Life was busy, but fun.

Only one problem marred our happiness. During a routine physical check-up, it was discovered that Norman was suffering from hypertension and latent-stage nephritis, a degenerative disease of the kidneys. The doctors didn't seem to know what had caused the condition, but it was thought that it might have occurred some years back when he was touring with the Cole circus.

He recalled having played on some lot up in Oregon and having been severely bitten by ticks. He had evidently developed an infection, and the nurse that traveled with the show treated him by putting pure sulfa on the wounds. The result was catastrophic, because he had an allergic reaction to the drug and blew up like a balloon. The only thing that saved him was the tattooed lady's insistence that he drink a lot of water.

Whether this was the inception really didn't matter. All that mattered was that he had it; and while there was no known cure for nephritis, it could, with proper medication and care, be kept under control. His high blood pressure and hypertension responded to medication, and at least Norm was able to function. A loss of weight would have really aided his general condition, but he loved to eat; and while he could rationalize the whole thing intellectually, he couldn't cope with it emotionally.

He decided that he wouldn't go on the road again, but he reckoned without the persuasiveness of John Ringling North. It was the summer of 1956, and Mr. North wanted Norman to come east to handle publicity.

I had never met the gentleman, but we were bombarded by a series of telephone calls, usually in the middle of the night. It seems from what I had heard, that Mr. North was a "night person" coming to life only after 6 p.m. This was all well and good except that little Kevin was an early riser; his waking time was 6 a.m., and those middle of the night interruptions of my sleep didn't do a thing for my disposition. After about four of those calls, I finally got up enough nerve to ask the gentleman to please call at a more respectable hour and told him why. The next call came at 9 p.m.!

Against Norman's better judgment, he decided to go and he also decided he would drive. He left early one morning, and the next thing I knew I received a call from Needles, California; it seems the car had broken down, and he was going to continue the trip by train. That meant that I had to take Kevin with me to Needles to pick up the car. Kevin seems to have been born with a one-track mind and that's a train track, so he was thrilled.

We spent the night in a hotel and in the morning went down to the garage to see how great the damage to the car might be. It turned out that all it had been was a vapor-lock. We got in, found it worked just fine, and drove all the way back to Los Angles without stopping.

In the meantime, Los Angeles was being treated to one of its periodic sieges of rain without a let-up. I found our basement flooded, and to make matters worse, Kevin developed a severe ear infection.

If all of this wasn't enough to drive me slightly mad; the next day, a show that I was handling was opening and I had to be there. I spent hours trying to get someone to sit with Kevin, but everyone either had colds or was bogged down in the rain. Fate works in strange ways, and just as I was despairing of ever getting to the opening of the show, I received a call from a friend of Norman's.

Rose Westlake had known Norm for many years, and they had toured together on the Cole show. At that time, she was Madam

Rose, the astrologer in the side show, but she had also been known as "Fifi, the Circassian Beauty" or "Fifi, the Sheepheaded Girl".

The "Circassians" (from Circassia, a region in Russia) were featured in side shows and were supposed to represent the purest white stock of the Caucasian race. Many of these were actually albinos who let their hair grow long and soaked it in stale beer to make it stand up. I doubt that Rose had to do that to her hair. She was a full-blooded Irish woman with extremely curly, kinky hair, and when she combed it in a certain way, it certainly met the going standards for Circassians. She was one of the most intelligent women I had ever met, and also one of the most knowledgeable. She and Norm would get into long, involved discussions about show business, politics or any subject, and they would sound like they were ready to kill each other at any moment, but there existed an understanding and a real bond between them.

Rose professed to hate "kids", but that day when she heard of my plight, the woman who hated children walked over five miles in pouring down rain and up a very steep hill to sit with Kevin.

Norman arrived in Chicago on July 16th, the town he was to start working in advance of the circus. His first afternoon there, he visited the Chicago Tribune only to be asked as he entered the City Room, "What are you doing here? Your show just closed!"

After the initial shock wore off, he read the wire service release saying that John Ringling North had closed the circus, adding that "the tented circus is a thing of the past." The world was shocked by the news, and the impression that most people got was that the circus was through forever.

Actually John Ringling North had said that "the circus, as we know it now, is a thing of the past, and new plans would be made for the circus in the future."

It was inevitable that something would have to happen to the circus. From its opening in New York at Madison Square Garden, it had been beset by labor trouble and had been picketed by the Teamsters Union and the American Guild of Variety Artists. While business had been pretty good at the start of the run, toward the end of the stand, it fell off badly.

When the show moved on to Boston, the unions staged a competing circus and charged a nominal admission with children admitted free. In addition to the union problems, the circus was plagued by railroad difficulties and a shortage of roustabouts.

Bad luck was following the show. In Geneva, New York, a sudden wind had ripped open the Big Top from end to end, injuring fifteen people. In several towns after that, performances were given without a tent, and others were canceled entirely. On July 15th, John Ringling North caught up with the show in Alliance Ohio, and after assessing the situation, dropped the bombshell the following day.

Ringling's great tented city was put up for the last time on a drab parking lot at the Heidelberg Raceway on the outskirts of Pittsburgh. Stunned performers gathered for the final matinee, and that night saw a capacity audience of 10,000, viewing the final performance.

It was not the end of the show if John Ringling North was to be believed. When the show closed in Pittsburgh, he had stated that it would open next season at Madison Square Garden as usual; but thereafter, it would be playing only in air-conditioned arenas.

The tented circus had been operating under conditions that were no longer practical. There was a real estate boom in most urban areas, and circus lots were becoming increasingly scarce. Also, the circus was in the hotel business with its 88-car train, and the restaurant business with its cookhouse that fed over a thousand people three times a day. With rising costs, the whole operation had to be revamped if it was to continue at all.

True to his word a new concept came into being. He would produce the circus and outside promoters would book the show into indoor arenas on a percentage basis. For the future Los Angeles engagements we would work with Feld Brothers, Irvin & Isadore, two very sharp men. They had made a fortune in the music business and eventually convinced John Ringling North to sell the circus to them.

Of course, all this didn't help Norman who was stranded in Chicago without a show. But it didn't take him long to make a decision; he was on the next train back to California.

CHAPTER FOURTEEN

John Ringling North was true to his word. On March 28, 1957, fifteen railroad cars, three sleepers, eight flats and four stock cars left Sarasota, Florida for the April 3rd opening in New York. Left behind were some sixty railroad cars, replaced by Ringling's new fleet of trucks.

Once again Norman left California to go east, this time to head up the radio and TV department of the circus. His doctor had been experimenting with some new drugs that were supposed to control high blood pressure, and he had been responding well for the short time he had been using them. So, it seemed safe for him to go.

I was involved in some motion picture and charity campaigns, and everything seemed to be going fine until shortly before the end of the New York engagement. On a Saturday afternoon at about 4 p.m., I received a telephone call from my brother in New York telling me that Norm was very ill and that I had better catch the next available plane for New York.

At the moment the call came in, we were just about to leave the house to attend a carnival at Kevin's nursery school. Naturally all plans were canceled while I tried to get a reservation for that night, arrange to turn my accounts over to someone else, close our house, and attend to all the million and one little details.

By 8 p.m., Kevin and I were on a plane heading east, and it was one of the most uncomfortable and longest flights I can ever remember taking. We were met at the airport by my brother and sister-in-law and drove directly to their house where Norman met us.

Poor darling was a nervous wreck and obviously very ill. We made plans to return home immediately. Norm was afraid to fly, so we had to reserve two bedrooms on the Super Chief, one to use as a sitting room and one to leave made up so that he could stay in bed.

I guess our visit to New York was one of the shortest on record; we arrived Sunday morning and left on Monday. It was only after our return to Los Angeles that we discovered that the reason for Norman's illness was due to the new medication; it had apparently backfired. Our little bout with that particular miracle drug cost us in the neighborhood of two thousand dollars.

Later in the year found us involved in the local campaign for the Ringling Brothers Circus in Los Angeles at the old Gilmore Stadium. Actually, it was the intention of the circus to play only air-conditioned indoor arenas, which were springing up all over the country; but some cities were a little behind schedule, and the Los Angeles Sports Arena had yet to be built, hence the ball park.

The Los Angeles engagement went all right, and then we were asked by the local promoter to help them with the campaign for the circus in Phoenix. They were having some trouble getting publicity breaks and needed a boost.

I had no one to leave Kevin with, and I wouldn't have considered doing so in any case, so we took him with us. I thought perhaps I could put him in a nursery school there while I made the rounds, but he'd have no part of it. Rather than create a traumatic situation for him, I decided that I would just take him with me, and he could wait for me in the reception rooms of the various radio and TV stations.

It was my job to get the circus story on the air in one way or another, so I was back to being interviewed as everything from the advance press agent to an aerialist.

One of the radio stations where I was scheduled to be interviewed also housed a TV studio. When we arrived there, I found that they did not have a receptionist, who was usually kind enough to keep a watchful eye on my son, but they did have a lobby which contained several chairs and a TV set.

I admonished Kevin not move but to watch TV until "mommy" returned and to be a good boy. With that I disappeared into the radio station for what turned out to be an half-hour interview. When I returned to the lobby, I was dismayed to find no Kevin. I was frantic, and my first thought was that someone had run off with him. There was no one around to ask if they had seen a small boy, and I was in a state of panic.

Just as I was about to head for the nearest phone to call the police to be on the lookout for a blond pixie, I happened to glance at the TV set, and just who, but my son, is staring back at me—not just sitting there, but big as life, plugging the coming engagement of the circus in as professional manner as I've ever heard.

The program was "Romper Room", and when the hostess arrived to do the show, she came through the lobby and discovered Kev. They struck up a conversation, and she was so enchanted with him that she asked him to appear on the show. No fool he; he agreed if she would let him talk about the circus!

On the subject of our son and his observations on the subject of publicity, when he was about six years old, the principal of Micheltorena Street School chose him to be one of four youngsters to represent the school on the Art Linkletter Show. If any of the readers have ever watched or listened to the "kids" on the show, they know they come out with the darndest things, so it was only natural that we would be pretty apprehensive about what *bon mot* our son might be apt to drop.

Our apprehension wasn't eased one bit when Kevin asked his father, "Gee, Dad, what can I say that will get a laugh?" Of course, that question occasioned a good half hour lecture about just being yourself, and never mind acting like a comedian; just act like a nice little boy.

We had worked with Art Linkletter on various projects for many years, and he knew we were in the audience and that Kevin belonged to us. I don't think I'm the stage mother type, but I sure had the jitters that day and couldn't wait for the whole thing to be over.

Art was his gracious, charming self, and when he came to Kevin, he said, "Now, this is a lucky little boy, his mother and father handle the publicity for Ringling Brothers and Barnum & Bailey

Circus, and he gets to go to the circus often." Then he turned to Kevin and added, "Kevin, would you like to go into the field of publicity when you grow up?" Whereupon our heir answered, "No, because all you do is lick envelopes!" Out of the mouths of babes . . . !

Instead of Art leaving it at that, he pursued, "Kevin, do you know what publicity is?" That elicited a "yes" answer, and Art asked Kevin to give the audience an example of publicity. That answer came out, "If mommy went to the hospital, and instead of a baby girl or boy, she came home with a Shetland pony, then we could take it down to the newspapers, and they would take its picture; and that would be publicity!"

After the show, when I could talk again, I asked Art if he had told Kevin to say that, and he said, "No, I thought you did." When we asked Kevin, he said he had thought that up all by himself, and what's more, it did get a laugh. Precocious kids, bah!

Actually, Kevin wasn't a precocious child, but from the time he was in nursery school and right through elementary, junior high and even high school, I've had to confront teachers who thought he was. If not precocious then he had a wild imagination.

It seems Kev, in all his innocence, would talk about having a lion in his basement, an elephant on the front lawn, or clowns in his living room, or his father announcing the circus, and his experiences around the circus. His teachers, not knowing that it was really the truth, were forever calling me to school for conferences.

CHAPTER FIFTEEN

Norman's health was a constant source of worry to us, but he was under the care of two fine doctors, and as long as he followed orders, he was able to function. Our life was busy and productive. Personally, we had a good standard of living. We had given up renting our little house when Kevin was five years old and bought an old house for a small sum. We then sold that house at a profit and bought a little better one, and so on through several until we owned a lovely townhouse high in the Hollywood Hills.

We were constantly busy what with the circus in late summer and several other shows in the spring and fall. Our son was growing into a fine young man, and when Christmas of 1964 rolled around, we felt we had much to be grateful for.

Christmas has always been our favorite holiday time, and this was an especially happy one because we loved our new home, and life was good. Norman's family and my mother celebrated the day with us, and we had just finished a huge dinner when, in the space of a few minutes, our lives changed radically.

Norman complained of pain in his chest and left arm, and at first, we thought it could be indigestion. He was way overweight, and he had just finished eating heartily. Rather than take a chance, we phoned the doctor who instructed us to take him to the hospital immediately. As it turned out, Norman had suffered a major coronary, and he was hospitalized for weeks, then confined to the house for a period of time. He seemed to make a remarkable recovery; and with the loss of weight, he looked younger and better than ever. He had a typical Irish baby face, and the weight loss was most becoming.

Fortunately, I was able to carry on our work, and to expedite matters, we had given up working at our regular office and had moved all our equipment into the downstairs of our home. What had been a bedroom became our office, and what was supposed to have been the garage now became a workroom, complete with carpet. In fact, we often joked about having the only carpeted garage in Hollywood! As far as I was concerned, this was ideal, I was at Norman's beckoned call, and we had the privacy that had been lacking in our other office.

It wasn't until late spring that Norman's doctor finally decided that he could go back to work full time. The timing was perfect because now it was almost time for the circus campaign to start full swing, and he was desperately needed.

1965 looked like it was going to be a record-breaking year for the circus. The advance was the largest yet in the Sports Arena, and the press couldn't have been more generous with space. Critics throughout the country had raved about the show and it looked like our hard work would pay off.

We opened on Wednesday, August 11th, with a matinee. One that saw the circus hosting over 10,000 underprivileged, orphans, and handicapped—including for the first time, blind children—as guests of the circus, and Norman, accepting a commendation from the Mayor.

At the night show, while it was open to the public, the circus hosted members of the press, radio and TV. There were civic and community leaders and entertainment personalities also in attendance. Everyone was enthusiastic in their praises of the show.

It was always our policy to leave after the intermission; mainly because by that time we were exhausted, having started our day at the crack of dawn with the circus unloading and TV shows.

Nothing seemed unusual in the parking lot when we went out to our car. But a few blocks from the Sports Arena, when we were about to turn onto the freeway, we noticed all kinds of military vehicles lined up on the off-ramp. We didn't give it too much thought because there was an armory located in that immediate vicinity, and we thought they might be practicing some kind of maneuvers. Little did we know at that time what kind!

It wasn't until the next day that we started hearing rumors about some unrest on the southeast side of town, but to us it still seemed somewhat remote, and we weren't concerned. Business was still good at the circus, although for the night performance, we began to get cancellation calls.

By Friday, it had gotten pretty scary. The heat was close to unbearable, and the general atmosphere of tension intensified even that. When we came off the freeway, near the Sports Arena, we could hear popping sounds, like a car backfiring. It wasn't until we reached the circus grounds that we found out what we had heard was a sniper perched on top of one of the buildings across from the Arena, taking pot shots at cars heading for the circus. Fortunately, he must have been a poor shot because we didn't hear of anyone actually being hurt. But it was one of the most frightening experiences I can ever remember.

To me, it was inconceivable to be standing in front of one of the newest and most beautiful buildings in the center of the City of Los Angeles, surrounded by policemen with drawn guns hunting down snipers. One almost got the feeling that they were watching a very bad "B" movie and that it was just too ludicrous for it to happen in real life.

What did happen is history. The Watts Riots—its causes, the events, the consequences—have been written and rewritten and probably will continue to be written until a final, positive solution to the problem is found. What hasn't been told is the effect that devastating event had on a small group of people—the people and the animals of the Greatest Show on Earth.

By Friday night, business had fallen off considerably, and people were glued to their TV sets. Saturday and Sunday were to be record-breaking days, if our advance was any indication, and it was decided to go ahead with the Saturday morning show, and play it from there.

Saturday morning found the situation worsening, and by now

fear was beginning to spread among the circus people. At first they hadn't been too aware, mainly because they weren't familiar with the locale, and then a good percentage of them were from foreign countries and did not speak English.

Attendance at the morning show was nil, and the circus officials decided it was just too dangerous to try to continue performances of the circus. The police hadn't actually declared the area off-limits, but it wasn't long in forthcoming. ,While the Sports Arena is not located in Watts—in fact, it is several miles from it—the area is considered a fringe area, and the large menagerie tent erected outside the arena in the Exposition Park area made the animals particularly vulnerable to any kind of attack.

I think everyone connected with the circus had just one thought. "What, if in all this insanity, some nut were to throw a match into all that straw?" The mental picture conjured up was just too horrible to contemplate. One could almost see twenty berserk and terrified elephants trampling everything in their wake, not to even speak of all the other animals.

Wild animals were kept inside the Arena, and they didn't present too much of a problem, but there wasn't enough room to bring all the elephants, horses, camels and assorted other animals inside. After many discussions, it was decided to hide the animals in an area under the huge Coliseum, and it was there that they and their fully-armed trainers stayed until the show was allowed to resume.

As for the performers, they were confined to the circus train which was located closer to the downtown area, still in a fringe area but not as volatile. Those performers who had cars would risk trouble by taking food to them and bringing many out to stay with circus friends in town. If we ever had the feeling of what it would be like to live in a "walled" city, this certainly gave us a good taste.

The circus remained closed for the weekend and Monday, but we were allowed to open on Tuesday. It was an eerie feeling to arrive on the circus lot and be greeted with the National Guard, fully armed, stationed every three feet, not only around the grounds but actually inside the circus.

Business dropped to a standstill, and trying to keep a campaign going under the circumstances was back-breaking work. We were both pushing ourselves to the limit, and after the Los Angeles date, we still had Long Beach to work.

The night of our last day in Long Beach, we had invited Henry Ringling North and his lovely wife to dinner at the Magic Castle, one of our accounts, an unusual private club for magicians in Hollywood. It was a time for relaxing and enjoying good company after the previous weeks. Norman was in fine fettle, full of jokes and his usual Irish charm; I was surprised when he whispered in my ear that he thought we had better leave. I knew better than to question him because if he wanted to leave, there had to be a good reason. We put our guests in the capable hands of a friend and departed.

Rather than dwell on all the unhappy details, Norman had suffered another, but even more devastating heart attack, and that was the beginning of the end.

At this point, all we could do was to try to get him well enough to meet with the principals of the circus when they came into town to negotiate the 1966 contract. Then, he would go back to bed, and I would carry on while Norman directed from the bedroom upstairs.

By the end of the 1966 engagement of the circus, Norm seemed to have made another amazing recovery, so much so that his doctor thought it would be all right for Kevin and I to go to Europe for a four-week trip. The morning we left, Norman felt fine, but he promised to behave himself and to be careful not to overdo. Evidently he couldn't keep his word because I found out later that we hadn't gotten as far as the airport before he was working in the garden and then later going out for lunches and dinners, and eating all the wrong foods.

We left on a Friday morning, and by Sunday night he was in intensive care at Cedars of Lebanon Hospital. It was decided not to let us know immediately, and it wasn't until half way through our trip, when we arrived in Rome, that we were advised of his condition. From that point on it was touch and go, and I saw the rest of Europe with half an eye. The final decision was that we were to come home on our regular flight. By the time we reached the hospital, coming directly from the airport, Norman had made another rally and was out of intensive care.

It is difficult to recall those last days, both in and out of the hospital. Norman was a remarkable man with a real zest for living. He was a perennial student and an avid reader, and as a final touch of irony, we found that he had developed a detached retina, and was blind in one eye.

I guess nature is kind to us because she has a way of making us blot out unhappy memories and only remember those that give us pleasure to recall. Such is the case with the events leading to the morning of Saturday, February 4th, when my beloved husband awakened me with the sound of his putting on the oxygen mask.

From that moment until forty-five minutes later at the hospital, when I said my final goodbye, I was grateful that he was not afraid of death. For Norman to have come to this point was a long, hard road. His early religious training and background had created fear of the unknown, and it was only in the last years that he had developed his understanding and acceptance of death.

Norman did not want a funeral, but I couldn't accede to his wishes on that score. He had a family and his Mother was still alive and Kevin wanted his father to have a funeral.

I chose a small cemetery in the heart of Westwood. Norman had always said he wanted to live in Westwood near the University; and I asked our dear friend, Ralph Story, to deliver the the eulogy. I knew this was asking a great deal of our friendship, but I just couldn't visualize someone who didn't really know Norman, talking about him. I think the following from Ralph's eulogy tells more that I ever could.

"It should be noted, and it is to the great credit of Norman Carroll, that a rather remarkable cross-section of humanity has gathered to honor him today. Few people could boast of such a diverse assortment of friends—and Norman didn't boast of them—

he simply welcomed them, enthused with them, complained with them, laughed with them and then said, 'come again, soon.' He was a very special person because he made all the rest of us feel so special. Maybe that's why we're all so sad today . . . we've lost a fellow who gave each of us importance . . . and today we've got to pay it back. You probably also noticed that the organ was not playing 'Abide with Me' or 'The Little White Church in the Vale' as you came in. It was playing show tunes instead . . . and that, too, was appropriate and fittingly requested by the family. Norman was in show business all his life . . . starting out as a clown in the circus. He was not a very good clown because he made all the other clowns laugh . . . and clowning is a very serious business. There wasn't—and still isn't—much future for a really good-natured, generous, warm-hearted clown, so he became a good-natured, generous, warm-hearted barker—sorry, 'outside talker' is the proper term. Norm was one of the great talkers, by any interpretation of those words.

"He talked his way into the Center Ring of the Greatest Show on Earth—and I noticed that most of the obituaries made special mention of his prominence as a Ringmaster. Actually, he did much more for the circus than that; he kept it alive in dark days, kept it on the road in lean times, helped to bring it up to date and make it a show, not just a tradition. He took the circus where it had never gone before—to hospitals and orphanages and asylums. It is Shirley's special pride that hundreds and hundreds of youngsters who had never seen a circus, and never would have, did, because of Norman. Even blind boys and girls saw the circus through his eyes. But it's even more surprising that he brought the circus to all of us who had seen it a hundred times. What was there about the strange sawdust pageant of the circus—so much like life and yet such a travesty of it—which captured the imagination and enthusiasm of Norman Carroll? Whatever it was, he passed it along, dispensed the magic and conjured the dreams like an outside talker.

"All the rest of the show business was his province and his pride, too. Wherever curtains go up tonight, they will wish he was there. Wherever there are lights and drama and talent on display, they will miss him. There will be fewer tickets and fewer tickled ribs, now that he's gone.

"And Norman's final resting place will be appropriate, too. In this oddly serene little oasis in the center of a chaotic community, there was very little space remaining. Providentially, perhaps, Shirley found an available plot right beside the center pathway of the cemetery. So our friend will have his favorite seat for eternity—'two on the aisle'.

"And now, with the humility of a stall act that has been on too long, before some good-natured generous clown shouts, 'get the hook, pull him off', I will just say that it is time for the teardown. The circus is over . . . "

During the services, Kevin peered out into the packed chapel where every seat was taken and where people were standing outside, then up at the wooden rafters. Finally, he turned to me and said, "You know mom, I have the feeling that Pop is sitting up there counting the house!"

If he was, he knew it was a "turnaway".

CHAPTER SIXTEEN

The days that followed Norman's death were like a dream and a rather bad one. Here I was with a fourteen year old boy, very little money because medical bills ate up what little reserve we had and the only insurance was a ten thousand dollar policy that Norm was able to get through the Publicist's Guild without having to pass a physical.

Thanks to his foresight, we did have a house and a car. The car was paid for and the mortgage on the house could be met as long as I was working. Fortunately, I was able to keep all our accounts—Ringling Brothers Circus, The Livestock and Dairy Show (the "Manure" shows), and the Magic Castle, Hollywood's famous private club for Magicians, and various others.

The 1967 season of the circus was a real trial. There was the move from the Sports Arena in Los Angeles to the Forum in Inglewood, and I needed a dramatic piece of artwork to make the announcement. Norman had always done the creative work, so confidence in my ability to come up with something effective was nil. Working with an artist and by trial and error and dumb luck, I finally did manage.

I was a wreck thinking about how I would cope with the arrival of the circus train and how I would handle all the press alone. Strange how fate plays a role in our lives. As it happened, on the day of the scheduled arrival, there was a train strike and by the time the train finally did arrive, I was so relieved to see it that I forgot how miserable I was going to feel!

I handled the circus in 1967, 1968, and 1969; but after the '69 engagement, I said, "Don't call me, I'll call you." The aggravation I had with the national press representative had taken its toll, and I realized that if I was going to be alive to see my son grow up, something had to go and it was the circus!

Of course, I might have had other thoughts if I had known that the "Manure" accounts were going to go down the drain at the same time,l but I still don't regret the decision. 1970 and part of 1971 were somewhat on the dismal side with my income cut substantially, but I managed to meet expenses.

As it turned out timing is everything. I had been busy running to my sister Gertrude's house to help because her husband was dying of cancer and she needed moral as well as physical help. I knew I should be out hustling up some new accounts, but I also knew that my sister and brother-in-law needed me, so I decided I would "let go and let God"; and that when I was ready, work would be there for me.

It's amazing when you release something to a higher power, it works! I wasn't quite ready, but I received a phone call from a young man, Brian Avnet, who was managing the rock opera "Tommy", written by the Who, at the Aquarius Theatre in Hollywood. It seems the press agent was ill and he wondered if I would cover for him for two weeks. I knew the press agent, and was happy to help him keep his job.

Brian invited me to come to see the show, and said he would leave two pair of tickets for me at the box office. I gave Kevin the tickets close to the stage and took the ones in the back of the house in case I couldn't stand it and wanted to get out.

Not only did I not want to get out but I was so thrilled with this new multi-media approach to theater and aside from not being able to hear for a week after the high decibel level, I was really enthusiastic. I found out the show hadn't received the greatest reviews when it opened but since that time had been reworked; however, it was scheduled to close shortly.

At the same time, I learned that the press agent wasn't sick but was on a drunken bender and that he had been fired. To hold that position, you had to be a member of the Association of Theatrical

Press Agents and Managers, and I fit that bill—having been a member for years—so the job was mine.

The first thing I did was to try to get the show reviewed again which was almost never done. I guess my enthusiasm was catching because I was successful, and the reviews were so good that the show ran an additional six months.

The reaction of the staff to this then 54-year old lady was an education. First of all, I walked around in a constant state of shock because every other word I heard spoken was a four-letter one. Finally one day I said to the stage manager, "Are you trying to shock me with that language?", and he was equally shocked that I took offense because to his generation, the words had a different meaning than they did to my generation. What was interesting is the day I got really angry about something and said "shit"; you would have thought the world stood still from his reaction!

Just before "Tommy" was scheduled to close, I received a call from Herb Steinberg at Universal Studios. I had worked with him on a circus promotion when he was at Paramount Studios and knew him to be a very fine man. He was now Public Relations Director for the tour and the new outdoor Amphitheater at Universal, and they were interviewing Union press agents for the production of "Jesus Christ Superstar" and he wanted to know if I would be interested in coming out for an interview.

When all the interviews were over, it boiled down to me and a long-haired, hippy looking young man who had submitted a great proposal. I didn't believe in proposals; I would rather have prospective clients check with current or past clients and the media to see if we delivered.

The result was that the young man got the account based on his proposal and that he had the current hippie look. One week later I received a call from the studio. It seems the proposal was great; but unfortunately, he couldn't deliver and would I be interested in being the press agent if I would agree to letting the young man work with me as an assistant.

It has always been my feeling that with age brings experience and knowledge that should be shared with youth, so of course, I agreed. He was a bright man and it was a pleasure to work with him. My agreement was that I would work on my other accounts from the office at the Studio and that I would bring my secretary, who was also my apprentice in the Union and that they would furnish the office, telephone and another secretary.

This was the beginning of my new life minus the circus. From "Tommy" to "Jesus Christ Superstar to "Rocky Horror Show, I became the oldest counter-culture publicist in the business.

The following year I was back at Universal—handling not only the Amphitheater that now featured all the great Rock artists plus the greats in the music business, but was asked to become the Director of Publicity for the Universal Tour and to move The Carrolls Agency, Inc. to the Studio. For eight delightful years, it was my home away from home.

My son married in 1979, and I decided it was time to leave the studio and move my office back into my home in the Hollywood Hills. Business was still good. I had three shows running at various theaters, including Henry Fonda in "Oldest Living Graduate", when I received a call from San Francisco.

A dear friend who was company manager on "Best Little Whorehouse in Texas" called because Labor Day was coming and she wanted me to come up for the weekend. Knowing that the show would be coming to Los Angeles in a few weeks and being busy with my work, I said no. A few hours later something made me call her back to say I was coming.

We had a great weekend; the Ringling Circus was at the Cow Palace and I took her and a few people from her show to see it. The following Sunday, I received a telephone call from her son to tell me she had had a heart attack and was dead! We were the same age and after the shock wore off, I took stock and said to myself "Stop the World, This is Where I Get Off!"

I had bought a small place in Laguna Hills some years before as an investment, never intending to retire; but now, I had to come to grips with the fact that I no longer needed to knock my brains out making a living. With my son married, I lived alone in a large house that was getting to be a burden. By the end of the year, I wound up my business, sold my house and moved to what has become the best decision of my life—retirement in what I consider paradise.

I am truly blessed with a daughter-in-law who is more than a daughter, two fantastic grandchildren, and my wonderful son. Believe it or not, they live right next to my gated community.

Many times over the years, people have commented about what a glamourous, exciting life I've led, and it did have its moments, but it was darn hard work that we tried to make look easy. Like the experience on the Cole Brothers Circus train, I wouldn't trade it for anything—but I sure wouldn't want to repeat it!

Printed in the United States
3072